A PRESERVING GRACE

MICHAEL CROMARTIE is a senior fellow and director of the Evangelical Studies Project at the Ethics and Public Policy Center in Washington, D.C. He is the editor of *Caesar's Coin Revisited: Christians and the Limits of Government*, of *Creation at Risk? Religion, Science, and Environmentalism*, and of other volumes.

A PRESERVING GRACE

Protestants, Catholics,
and Natural Law

Edited by
MICHAEL CROMARTIE

ETHICS AND PUBLIC POLICY CENTER
WASHINGTON, D.C.

WILLIAM B. EERDMANS PUBLISHING COMPANY
GRAND RAPIDS, MICHIGAN

Published jointly 1997 by the Ethics and Public Policy Center and
Wm. B. Eerdmans Publishing Co.
255 Jefferson Ave. S.E., Grand Rapids, Mich. 49503

Library of Congress Cataloging-in-Publication Data

A preserving grace: Protestants, Catholics, and natural law /
edited by Michael Cromartie.
p.   cm.
Includes bibliographical references and index.
ISBN 0-8028-4306-9 (paper: alk. paper)
1. Natural law — Religious aspects. 2. Natural law.
I. Cromartie, Michael.
K460.P74   1997
171'.2 — dc21   96-48112
CIP

Contents

Preface   vii
    Michael Cromartie

1 *Natural Law and Catholic Moral Theology*   1
Russell Hittinger
    A Response   31
      Carl E. Braaten
    Comments   41

2 *Calvin's Use of Natural Law*   51
Susan E. Schreiner
    A Response   77
      Timothy George
    Comments   84

3 *The Reformed Tradition and Natural Law*   103
Daniel Westberg
    A Response   118
      William Edgar
    Comments   131

4 *The Concept of Rights in Christian
Moral Discourse*   143
Joan Lockwood O'Donovan

A Response   157
  Robert P. George
Comments   162

Appendix: *Conference Participants*   173

Notes   175

Index of Names   191

Preface

Some Protestants run the danger of treating the Bible like a wax nose that can be twisted any way one pleases, remarked the Spanish cardinal Merry del Val. The same could be said about the way many Protestants—and non-Protestants—treat the concept of natural law. According to this concept, there is a universal law to which people of all races, cultures, and religions can have access through their natural reason. Natural law provides ethical and moral standards that all persons can grasp without the aid of special divine revelation. But the theory remains a point of controversy among theologians, political philosophers, and legal theorists, Christian and non-Christian alike.

Yet there is growing evidence of renewed interest in the role that a revived natural law theory might play in political discourse. When moral concerns such as abortion are debated in the public arena, the debate is often hampered by the lack of a moral vocabulary acceptable to both religious and secular interlocutors. Could such a common moral grammar be found in the Christian natural law tradition? Why have Protestants been so critical of natural law theory when there is considerable evidence that the Reformers considered natural law a part of the divine law? And why is there an apparent gulf between what Thomas Aquinas meant by natural law and what many modern Catholic philosophers mean by it?

These were some of the questions in the air in March 1996 when the Ethics and Public Policy Center's Evangelical Studies Project brought together a diverse group of Protestant and Catholic scholars to explore Christian approaches to natural law. For a day and a half more than twenty philosophers, theologians, and political scientists engaged in a vigorous and stimulating exchange centered on papers by Russell Hittinger, formerly professor of philosophy at Catholic

University, who now holds the Warren Chair of Catholic Studies at the University of Tulsa; Susan E. Schreiner, associate professor of church history at the University of Chicago; Joan Lockwood O'Donovan, a political philosopher from Oxford, England; and Daniel Westberg, assistant professor of religious studies at the University of Virginia. Each paper was followed by a response from a distinguished commentator. In addition to these eight essays, this volume includes comments made by the speakers and more than a dozen other participants (identified on pages 173-74) in the lively discussion that ensued.

Russell Hittinger notes in his essay that "within Roman Catholic theology, the *existence* of natural law is not very controversial." What has caused disagreements, he says, is the differing emphases theorists give to its "three foci": "natural law in the human mind, in things or nature, and in divine providence." While Thomas Aquinas emphasized that "natural law is divine law" and never defined its precepts, subsequent commentators have focused increasingly on the independent power of human cognition to discern "what all men know." This modern preoccupation with reason and certainty, Hittinger argues, has tended to divorce natural law from the "divine lawgiver" and to reduce it to little more than a means for settling moral disputes and guiding personal conduct. In the recent encyclicals *Evangelium Vitae* and *Veritatis Splendor,* however, Pope John Paul II, according to Hittinger, "gets the problem of natural law situated just about right." Respondent **Carl Braaten**, a Lutheran theologian who is executive director of the Center for Catholic and Evangelical Theology, applauds Hittinger's efforts to re-establish the critical link between natural law and theology and maintains that "law without higher authority becomes lawless." Braaten argues that when Martin Luther appropriated the concept of natural law from Catholicism, while he transformed it he never divorced it from divine providence. Natural law, in the Lutheran tradition—evident in the "orders of creation"—is one mode of God's activity in the world, preparing "the way for the good news of divine grace" as revealed in the Gospel.

Susan Schreiner notes that John Calvin's use of natural law has been "a hotly disputed topic in Calvin studies since the beginning of this century." After surveying the core issues of the debate, she argues that Calvin himself did not see his appeals to natural law as problematic. Students of Calvin's thought have questioned how the corrupted human mind and the depraved human nature that he describes can have any natural knowledge of God's will. The answer to this conundrum, Schreiner suggests, lies in Calvin's doctrine of divine providence, a providence that has sustained nature and society since man, through Adam's sin, plunged the world into chaos. God has prevented complete disorder and anarchy through the restraint of the "moral law," which Calvin defined as "that natural law and . . . that conscience which God has engraved upon the minds of men." In Calvin's thought, the "bridle of divine providence" curbs people "lest they devour one another." The human ability to discern the natural law through human conscience is a preserving grace whereby a semblance of order, stability, and beauty is maintained. Respondent **Timothy George**, the dean of Beeson Divinity School, wonders whether it is possible to "extrapolate out of Calvin a doctrine of natural law that can serve as a grammar of public discourse today without doing violence to his own intentions." Calvin may have found natural law useful to some degree, says George, but his theological doctrine as a whole seemed to say that "at best, natural law might provide a kind of negative incentive for ministers of divine justice."

Daniel Westberg observes that, despite current efforts to revive natural law, some Protestants remain reluctant to "compromise with a doctrine of moral standards based on human nature or reason" that they associate with a deeply flawed tradition of Roman Catholic moral theology. But he suggests that while Catholic natural law theory is a "handy target," this negative posture does not take into account "the errors and exaggerated claims for natural law that arose in later Protestant versions." These errors explain in part the suspicion that remains among many Protestants today. Westberg points out some of these weaknesses of later Protestant versions of natural law as he surveys the views of prominent Reformed theologians John Calvin, Heinrich Bullinger, William Ames, Hugo Grotius, and Emil Brunner. Respondent **William Edgar**, a professor of apologetics at Westminster Theological Seminary, elaborates on the unfortunate evolution of natural law that Westberg describes: the transformation of the more limited theories of Calvin into the inflated and mechanistic dogma advanced by later religious and philosophical thinkers. Edgar argues that natural law for Calvin had been "indissolubly connected to God's authority" but by the nineteenth century had become a "semi-autonomous principle perceivable by unaided reason." He cautions adherents of natural law to refuse to "forge social programs that confuse amelioration with salvation. We need to avoid social Pelagianism."

Joan Lockwood O'Donovan critiques the modern concept of natural and subjective rights, which is firmly entrenched in the political and legal discourse of our day. Lamenting that theologians often engage in "a naïve and facile appropriation of the language of rights," she finds this "an undesirable element of contemporary Christian moral discourse, and . . . problematic within an evangelical or Christological approach to natural law." O'Donovan provides a historical survey of the concept of subjective rights and finds a "progressive antagonism between the older Christian tradition of political right and the newer voluntarist, individualist, and subjectivist orientation." Respondent **Robert George**, a professor of politics at Princeton University, shares O'Donovan's mistrust of modern liberalism but argues that it is liberalism's understanding of human beings and human motivation, rather than its concept of rights, that makes it "incompatible with Christianity." Though moral principles, not rights, play the foundational role in Christian philosophy, claims of right are no more inherently selfish and un-Christian than claims of justice, says George. "Claims of right are either true or false; our goal is to affirm the claims that are true and deny the false ones."

I would like to thank several colleagues at the Ethics and Public Policy Center. Over the years, I have written so many encomiums to the skills of Senior Editor Carol Griffith that I fear repeating myself. Suffice it to say that her superb editorial work and always sage advice are deeply appreciated. Ethan Reedy rendered diligent assistance, always with good cheer and high competence; besides helping to organize the conference, he did heroic work in transcribing tapes and typing the manuscript. Ann Derstine, Chris Ditzenberger, and Marianne Geers also helped with the manuscript, and their work is appreciated.

The Ethics and Public Policy Center's statement of purpose says in part that the Center strives "to deepen and broaden public debate on the ordering of our society and its relationship to the rest of the world." At all our conferences it is our express purpose to have diverse viewpoints expressed and "to foster a wiser moral and political debate across ideological barricades." The issues addressed in this volume are "pre-political"; they have to do with the differing theoretical assumptions that underlie much of our political discord. We hope that this book will encourage constructive thinking and fresh dialogue among Protestants, Catholics, and the many others, both religious and nonreligious, who want to strengthen the influence of moral values in our common life.

MICHAEL CROMARTIE

1

Natural Law and Catholic
Moral Theology

Russell Hittinger

In his 1958 lectures at the University of Chicago, later published under the title *The Tradition of Natural Law: A Philosopher's Reflections,* Yves R. Simon remarks that the subject of natural law is difficult "because it is engaged in an overwhelming diversity of doctrinal contexts and of historical accidents. It is doubtful that this double diversity, doctrinal and historical, can so be mastered as to make possible a completely orderly exposition of the subject of natural law."[1]

My intention in this essay will be to examine the problem of natural law only *ad intra,* within Catholic moral theology.[2] The essay will have almost nothing to say about any particular issue of justice in the public sphere. It will proffer no "natural law" answers as to what judges ought to do, or how the budget deficit ought to be resolved, or what moral perspective should guide welfare funding. Furthermore, although it might reinforce the suspicion of evangelical Protestants that

Russell Hittinger holds the Warren Chair of Catholic Studies at the University of Tulsa, Oklahoma, where he is also a research professor of law. He previously taught philosophy at The Catholic University of America in Washington, D.C., and was a research fellow at the American Enterprise Institute. Among his books is *A Critique of the New Natural Law Theorists* (University of Notre Dame Press, 1989).

1

there is something both attractive and repellent about Catholic uses of natural law, it will not try to convince Protestants on any specific disputed issue.

Rather, I will endeavor to show how the concept of natural law became a serious problem in modern Catholic moral theology, and how the papal encyclical *Veritatis Splendor* responds to that problem. My account will be very imperfect indeed, for it will be necessary both to tell a story and to make a number of distinctions along the way, allowing each to illuminate the other. To do both these things at once, and in a brief space, is a difficult task.

Three Foci of Natural Law Discourse

But first, what is a theory of natural law a theory *of?* The question can be approached in three ways. In the first place, natural law can be regarded as a matter of propositions or precepts that are first in the order of practical cognition. Thus, when a theorist reconnects debate about justice back to first principles, from which the mind can lay out properly considered and argued conclusions, he can be said to have (or practice) a theory of natural law. In the second place, natural law can be regarded as an issue of nature or human nature, in which case it is a problem not only of epistemology and logic but also of how practical reason is situated in a broader order of causality. Third, natural law can be approached not only as order in the mind or order in nature but also as the ordinance of a divine lawgiver.

Discourse about natural law can gravitate toward any one or a combination of these three foci: law in the human mind, in nature, and in the mind of God. Contemporary literature on the subject shows there is little or no agreement as to how the three foci ought to be integrated. For there is no general agreement about what should count as a proper problem, much less about what philosophical instruments to apply to it.

Rather than engage in an interminable survey of the methodological problems, I shall begin with an assertion. The theologian is (or ought to be) chiefly concerned with the third of these foci: namely, natural law as an expression of divine providence. As Karl Barth said in *Church Dogmatics,* "Ethics [is] a Task of the Doctrine of God."[3] Whatever else Barth said or thought about natural law, the proposition that moral theology is a task of the doctrine of God is incontestable. The Christian theologian is interested in who God is, and what God does, as he reveals himself.

Who we are and what we do are questions that can be asked outside of theology, to be sure, and the theologian will be interested in how persons outside the faith pursue such questions. Catholic and Protestant theologians have different attitudes toward these strands (Balthasar says "fragments") of moral inquiry and behavior separated from the living Word of God. While Catholic theologians have perhaps been tempted to overestimation, Protestants have been inclined to underestimation. But the main focus for the theologian *qua* theologian is, as Barth said, the doctrine of God.

HISTORICAL REFLECTIONS

Until recently, the proposition that natural law is chiefly a theological issue was uncontroversial in Catholic moral theology. Natural law in the human mind and natural law in nature were regarded as distinct but not architectonic foci. Let us first consider two passages from the Church Fathers.

In the second century, Tertullian took up the problem of divine governance prior to the written law. Like so many other of the patristic theologians of both east and west, Tertullian argued that the law given to Adam (Gen. 2:17) was the natural law: "For in this law given to Adam we recognize in embryo all the precepts which afterwards sprouted forth when given through Moses." After reciting the ten precepts of the Decalogue, Tertullian concludes that the first law is "the womb of all the precepts of God"—a "law unwritten, which was habitually understood naturally, and which the fathers kept."[4] Which of the patriarchs? Tertullian mentions Noah, Melchizedek, Enoch, and Abraham.

This teaching is simple and familiar. Our first parents were given an unwritten law, expressing the rule of law itself: men govern only by sharing in divine governance. Adam and Eve, who understood the law *naturaliter* (naturally), did not keep it. But the patriarchs before Moses adhered to the unwritten law. In this brief passage Tertullian alludes to natural law in the mind and in nature. His principal interest,

however, is the economy of divine laws. As to what men knew or did *post peccatum,* Tertullian commits himself only to saying that the patriarchs were counted "righteous, on the observance of a natural law."[5]
In the fourth century, Gregory of Nyssa proposed:

> . . . that human nature at its beginning was unbroken and immortal. Since human nature was fashioned by the divine hands and beautified with the unwritten characters of the Law, the intention of the Law lay in our nature in turning us away from evil and in honoring the divine. When the sound of sin struck our ears, that sound which the first book of Scripture calls "the voice of the serpent," but the history concerning the tables calls the "voice of drunken singing," the tables fell to the earth and were broken. But again the true Lawgiver, of whom Moses was a type, cut the tables of human nature for himself from our earth. It was not marriage which produced for him his "God-receiving" flesh, but he became the stonecutter of his own flesh, which was carved by the divine finger, for *the Holy Spirit came upon the virgin and the power of the Most High overshadowed her.* When this took place, our nature regained its unbroken character, becoming immortal through the letters written by his finger.[6]

Like Tertullian, Gregory of Nyssa alludes to natural law in the mind. The "intention of the Law," he writes, "lay in our nature in turning us away from evil and in honoring the divine." This is the traditional notion of a *lex indita,* a law instilled in the mind, which later patristic and medieval theologians would call *synderesis.*[7] Gregory also speaks of the order of human nature. Yet it is clear that Gregory's focus is set upon what God does: first in ordering man by nature, second in disciplining men through the written law, and finally in recreating men through the mystery of the Incarnation and Redemption.

These two passages are typical of the patristic thinking on natural law. Issues of epistemology and human nature are distinct but not architectonic foci. Not even moral theology (in our modern sense) is the main focus. Rather, theology proper, the doctrine of revelation, organizes the Fathers' perspective. Chief among the theological themes are (1) the economy of divine laws, (2) the manner in which Christ recapitulates not just Moses but Adam, and (3) generally, getting the story right, which is to say, thinking rightly about Scripture.[8]

As early as the Second Council of Arles (473), the "law of nature" *(lex naturalis)* was defined as "the first grace of God."[9] Beginning in late antiquity, theologians transformed the nomenclature of the lawyers to bring it in line with Christian theology. The Corpus Iuris Civilis divided law generally into *ius naturale, ius gentium,* and *ius civile.*[10] The word *lex* was not reserved for written law (according to the *Institutes of Justinian, scriptum ius est lex*) but was especially associated with imperial pronouncements.[11] The Lex Julia, for example, was the Julian Act.[12] This usage was also adopted by the canonists. *Lex,* Gratian states in the *Decretum,* is a written statute, a *constitutio scripta;* and a *constitutio,* he goes on to explain, is "what a king or emperor has decided or declared."[13] In St. Thomas's *Summa Theologiae,* the *iura* are classified as *leges.* So, rather than the *ius naturale,* we get not only *lex naturalis* but a classification of law according to diverse *leges,* such as *lex aeterna, lex nova, lex Mosaicae, lex membrorum, lex humana,* and *lex vetus.*[14] The term *lex,* which the lawyers reserved for a written edict issued by an imperial lawgiver, had become for theologians a usage emphasizing the divine origin of all law, whether it be instilled in the heart or imparted by written or oral arts.

As regards the being and cause of the natural law, the theological tradition moved steadily away from any anthropocentric or merely naturalistic conception of the *ius naturale.*[15]

Misperceptions of Thomas

The thought of Thomas Aquinas has, of course, become nearly synonymous with "Catholic" doctrine of natural law. It would take volumes to dispel the modern misperceptions and misrepresentations of his natural law theory. Many misperceptions are due to the fact that Thomas, more than the patristic theologians, articulated the epistemological and natural foci with some philosophical precision. Those discussions in Thomas are often lifted out of context and debated as if they were completely independent of theology.

I have no intention of trying to dispel all these misperceptions at their proper level of detail and complexity. Two general points, however, need to be made. First, nowhere does Thomas *define* natural law in anything but theological terms. Indeed, in answer to the objection that for there to be both an eternal law and a natural law was needless duplication, Thomas responds: "this argument would hold if the natural law were something diverse from the eternal law, whereas it is nothing but a participation thereof."[16] Natural law is never (and I must emphasize *never*) defined in terms of what is first in the (human) mind or first in nature.[17]

Although his modern readers have little inclination to discriminate among the three foci—natural law in the mind, in nature, in the mind of God—or to reflect upon their order of priority, Thomas understood what is at stake in arriving at a proper definition. The fact that we first perceive ourselves discovering or grasping a rule of action does not mean that the human mind is first in the causal order, or in the ultimate order of being. For example, the judge who discovers a rule does not equate the cause of discovery with the cause of the rule—unless, perchance, they are one and the same. In the case of natural law, Thomas defines the law from the standpoint of its causal origin (that is, what makes it a law), not in terms of a secondary order of causality through which it is discovered (the human intellect).

Without the order of priority, we have either nature or the human mind as the cause of the law—not the cause of knowing or discovering, but the cause of the law itself. This would destroy the metaphysical continuity between the various dispensations of divine providence. For if God is to govern, he will have to supersede, if not destroy, the jurisdiction constituted (allegedly) by human causality. Insofar as the natural law is regarded as the foundation of the moral order, and insofar as that is thought to be caused (and not merely discovered) in some proper and primary way by human cognition, God will have to unseat the natural law. Almost all the modern theories of natural law seek to relieve that conflict in favor of what is first in the human mind. Thomas understood what is at stake in giving definitions, and was exceedingly careful not to confuse what is first in human cognition with what is first in being.[18]

In the second place, as we saw earlier, Tertullian used the adverb *naturaliter* (naturally) not to characterize the law but rather to describe how it is known. Nature is not the law but the mode of knowing it. This Latin adverb would eventually find its way into the Vulgate translation of Romans 2:14-15 to characterize what the gentiles know or do without benefit of divine positive law. Thomas Aquinas frequently uses the same term in order to emphasize the mode of divine promulgation.[19] Natural law is *lex indita,* instilled in the human mind by God, moving the creature to its proper acts and ends. As for his estimation of the efficacy of natural law in the human mind, Thomas never wavered from the judgment that only the rudiments (or the *seminalia,* the seeds) are known by the untutored mind. With regard to the gentiles mentioned in Romans 2:14, those "who having not the Law, did naturally [*naturaliter . . . faciunt*] things of the Law," St. Thomas points out that the words *naturaliter* and *faciunt* indicate that St. Paul was referring to gentiles whose "nature had been reformed by grace [*per naturam gratia reformatam*]." Any other interpretation, Thomas warns, would be Pelagian.[20]

Thomas is well known for having insisted upon the *de jure* possibility of affirming the existence of God by natural reason. His estimation of the *de facto* condition of the human mind led him to make the cautious statement "known by a few, and that after a long time, and with the admixture of many errors."[21] More to the point, however, Thomas explicitly and emphatically denied that the philosophers were able to translate such scraps of theology into virtuous acts of religion. None of the pagan theologies satisfied the natural, not to mention supernatural, virtue of religion.[22]

In his last recorded remarks on the subject of natural law, made during a series of Lenten conferences in 1273, Thomas's judgment is even more stern: "Now although God in creating man gave him this law of nature, the devil oversowed another law in man, namely, the law of concupiscence. . . . Since then the law of nature was destroyed by concupiscence, man needed to be brought back to works of virtue, and to be drawn away from vice: for which purpose he needed the written law." As the critical Leonine edition of 1985 confirms, the words are *destructa erat*—"was destroyed."[23]

How can he say that natural law is destroyed in us? First, he certainly does not mean that it is destroyed in the mind of the lawgiver. As a law, natural law is not "in" nature or the human mind, but is rather in the mind of God. The immutability of natural law, he insists, is due to the "immutability and perfection of the divine reason that institutes it."[24] Insofar as natural law can be said to be "in" things or nature, it is an order of inclinations of reason and will by which men are moved to a common good. While the created order continues to move men, the effect of that law (in the creature) is bent by sin—not so bent that God fails to move the finite mind, for the fallen man is still a spiritual creature, possessed of the God-given light of moral understanding, but bent enough that this movement requires the remediation of divine positive law and a new law of grace.[25] In fact, Thomas held that God left men in such a condition —between the time of the Fall and the Mosaic law—in order to chastise them.[26] The so-called "time of natural law," which refers, of course, to the historical and moral condition of man, not the precepts of the natural law itself, is not normative for Thomas's ethics. And it is the effort to *make* that condition normative that marks the modern project.

By Thomas's day, natural law theory was being used in debates over jurisdiction between civilians and canonists; it was also being used on at least a partial basis for trying to get right answers about disputed matters of personal conduct. But in Thomas there is little of this. There is only one sustained discussion, extending over several articles, in which Thomas subjects a disputed issue of personal conduct to what could be called a natural law analysis. It is from the very beginning of his career, when he was still a graduate student, in his exposition of the *Sentences of Peter Lombard*. This exposition, which is now appended to the *Summa* and called the "Supplement," contains an extended natural law argument on the problem of polygamy.

Interestingly, the problem was one he could not resolve by using natural law. Thomas ends up saying that polygamy violates no first precept of the natural law. With the ordering of sex to procreation, the polygamist does not violate the natural law. The remainder of Thomas's argument was a tentative one, namely, that polygamy made social life inconvenient, and that it would be difficult for the society of husband and wife to maintain itself properly intact in that kind of an arrangement. His only decisive argument against polygamy is sacramental—Jesus cannot have plural churches, man cannot have plural wives. And so the one serious effort he made to resolve the kind of issue we talk about today—a disputed moral issue—ended somewhat inconclusively on the natural law note. Once he reached that stalemate, he quickly reverted to sacramental theology as a way of resolving the issue.

Eclipse of the Theology

In the modern era, the theology of natural law was moved to the periphery, and was usually eclipsed altogether. The epistemological and natural foci become architectonic. The new sciences adopted the method of resolutive analysis and compositive synthesis. Under this method, the appearances of nature are analytically reduced to the most "certain," which is to say, the most predictable, elements: namely, modes of quantity, such as size, shape, and velocity. Then, through compositive synthesis, the quantities can be rebuilt as mathematical objects. This method was applied beyond physics to humane matters. In *De Homine*, for example, Hobbes takes man as he is, a thing of "meer nature," and reduces the appearances to stable and predictable modes of quantity. Once we have done this, we do not find Presbyterians and Catholics; rather, we find a stimulus-response mechanism that endeavors to augment its power. What is first, then, is natural laws as "lower" laws rendering men amenable to the law of the sovereign. In *De Cive,* man is rebuilt according to rules that are true laws. Hobbes explains: "Politics and ethics (that is, the sciences of just and unjust, of equity and inequity) can be demonstrated *a priori;* because we ourselves make the principles—that is, the causes of justice (namely, laws and covenants)—whereby it is known what justice and equity, and their opposites injustice and inequity, are."[27]

Hobbes, of course, was a materialist. But this method of reduction and recomposition was not tied to materialist doctrines. Continental rationalism and idealism also deployed methods of reduction to what is first in the mind, from which reality can be constructed, modeled, predicted. In the reduction, Hobbes could find only "lower" laws; other Enlightenment thinkers purported to find first principles of justice and equity. Whatever the differences, the trademarks are certainty and predictability, gauged according to what is first in cognition.

Yet the main reason for the eclipse of the theology of natural law was the theologico-political problem. What better way to solve such a problem than to imagine men's appealing to no authority other than what is first in the mind? Virtually all of the Enlightenment "state of nature" scenarios make this move. In Hobbes, Locke, Rousseau, and Kant, man is considered in an "original" position, under the authority of no pope, prince, or scripture. If there is a God, he governs through no mundane authority. Authority will have to make its first appearance in the covenants of individuals constrained to reach a consensus on the basis of what is (or seems) self-evident. The twelfth-century summist Johannes Faventinus declared: "The streams of natural rectitude flow into the sea of natural law, such that what was lost in the first man is regained in the Mosaic law, perfected in the Gospels, and decorated in human customs."[28] The modern myth of the "state of nature" rejects this scheme of divine pedagogy—not directly, but indirectly, by rendering it superfluous to the quest for first principles of the political order. Indeed, the "state of nature" was meant to be a secular substitute for the story of Genesis. Never a pure science of morality, it was rather a merely useful one, designed for the political purpose of unseating the traditional doctrine of natural law.

The fact that a proposition is pellucid, knowable without logical need of a middle term (e.g., "life is good," which can be grasped without a set of theological inferences or authorities), is supposed reason enough to conclude that logical independence means ontological independence; and the "state of nature" mythology had the aim of representing that independence. Since no orthodox Christian theology holds that God and his orders of providence and of salvation crop up as what is first in untutored cognition, to force natural law into that one understanding is bound to destroy moral theology on the reefs of half-truth. The half-truth is that there are principles of practical cognition that are proximate to the natural functioning of the intellect. But they are only the beginning (the *seminalia*) of practical reason. When the starting points are made autonomous, the human mind declares independence not only from the deeper order of divine tutoring but also from the tutoring afforded by human culture, including human law.

This is why natural rights, for so many modern advocates, turn out to be nothing other than immunities against the order of law. Thus, what began for the Christian theologians as a doctrine explaining how the human mind participates in a higher order of law is turned into its opposite. The natural law becomes "temporal," the temporal becomes "secular," and the secular becomes the sphere in which human agents enjoy immunity from any laws other than those they impose upon themselves.

For a time, Catholics were not confused by the new ideologies of natural law, for these conceptions were expressed by political movements vehemently hostile to the Church. But once political modernity became the "normal" state of affairs, and once the Church found a way to respond to modernity in something more than a purely reactive mode, it was almost inevitable that the new conceptions of natural law would begin to color moral theology.

MODERN CATHOLIC THOUGHT

There is a superficial congruity between the tradition of Catholic moral theology and modernity. Both (in various ways) hold that there is a moral order first in the mind, and that some problems can be reasoned without immediate introduction of premises drawn either from revelation or from a fully worked-out cosmology of nature. The overlap of traditions on this specific point is apt to be misleading. Thomist, Cartesian, and Kantian conceptions of what it means to be "first" in the mind express very different understandings of practical reason, and how practical reason is situated with regard to what is "first" in nature and in ultimate order of being.

But when the focus on what is first in the mind is conjoined with the desperate modern need for consensus, it becomes easy for Catholic uses of natural law theory to cross over into something new. The use of natural law by moral theologians has always been Janus-faced. Natural law can be used to express specifically theological propositions about divine providence, or it can be used to ground or mount arguments about particular disputed issues of conduct.

In modern times, we observe a steady drift toward the latter use, and with it a gradually diminishing sense of the sapiential context afforded by theology proper. Nowhere can this be seen more clearly than in the tradition of modern social encyclicals. As to things that have been declared contrary to nature and/or reason, a short list includes: dueling, Communism, divorce, contraception, Freemasonry, *in vitro* fertilization, and contract theories of the origin of political authority. And this is not to mention the bevy of rights and entitlements that have been declared to be owed to persons under the rubric of justice *ex ipsa natura rei,* by the very nature of the thing. Read carefully, the encyclicals assume that all three foci (law in the mind, in things, and decreed by divine providence) are legitimate and in principle are integrated in moral theology. Compared to his successors, Leo XIII was especially careful to make the distinctions that kept divine providence in the picture.[29]

Natural Law as a Persuasive Tool

It is not my intention to cast doubt on any particular assertion about natural law or natural rights in these official documents. The problem (for our purposes here) is not particular judgments about the morality of dueling or contraception, but the possibility that the encyclical uses of natural law create the misleading impression that on any vexed issue the minds of the faithful and the gentiles can be adequately directed by appeal to elementary principles of natural law. The moral picture of a baptized agent becomes difficult to distinguish from that of the unbaptized, which is not surprising, since so many of the encyclicals deal with political and economic crises. Thus we have the Church reaching into its treasury of wisdom and pulling out the right answer without adequately displaying the wisdom, and sometimes without showing how the chain of arguments is grounded in anything other than church authority.

Humanae Vitae suffered especially in this regard. Some rather thin strands of argument about natural functions are terminated in one direction in the Church's authority to interpret the natural law. Not surprisingly, Pope John Paul II has devoted much of his pontificate to filling out the picture, beginning with a book-length set of allocutions on the proper exegesis of Genesis.

In any case, the teaching method of trimming arguments to fit what is first in cognition, buttressed perhaps with appeals to what is first in the chain of legal command (the papal office), would eventually yield diminishing and disappointing results, not only for the gentiles but also for the faithful—especially the moral theologians. By almost imperceptible steps, it was easy to fall into the habit of regarding discourse about natural law as an instrument of persuasion, the truth of which becomes measured by its success in garnering assent.

Take, for example, Cardinal Maurice Roy's 1973 remarks on the "Occasion of the Tenth Anniversary of the Encyclical 'Pacem in Terris.'" Addressing himself to Pope Paul VI, Cardinal Roy has this to say about the encyclical's references to natural law:

Although the term "nature" does in fact lend itself to serious mis-understandings, the reality intended has lost nothing of its force-fulness when it is replaced by modern synonyms. . . . Such syn-onyms are: man, human being, human person, dignity, the rights of man or the rights of peoples, conscience, humaneness (in con-duct), the struggle for justice, and, more recently, "the duty of being," the "quality of life." Could they not all be summarized in the concept of "values," which is very much used today?[30]

Interestingly, on John XXIII's remark that peace is "absolute respect for the order laid down by God,"[31] Roy observes: "But here again, this word jars the modern mentality, as does, even more, the idea that it summons up: a sort of complicated organic scheme or gigantic genealogical tree, in which each being and group has its predetermined place." Eager to reinforce truths proximate to the human mind (or, perhaps, those least proximate to the chain of church authority), Roy seemed to find even the phrase "order laid down by God" too theo-logically strong. Whereas earlier generations of theologians addressed the gentiles by emphasizing the relationship between moral order and divine providence, a new generation of Catholic theologians was being taught (inadvertently) that the rudiments of moral order ought to be discussed without any reference to divine governance, or, for that matter, to created nature. Modern gentiles, it seems, cannot bear the burden of even the weakest theological discourse.

To give credit where it is due, it must be said that the Church was thrust into the position of having to teach, *ad extra*, about precepts of the moral order that are in principle proximate to the human mind. That nations or individuals must not murder, must not rape, and must not plunder are not uniquely theological propositions. Many of the precepts advanced in papal encyclicals have been held by men of good will who do not explicitly assent to Christian doctrines. The Catholic Church has always regarded itself as a consensus-builder among the peoples and nations.

Seizing the Post-War Moment

The high tide of the overestimation of natural law discourse was the post–World War Two era, when the Church was eager to reinforce the right lessons of the war. Western modernity found itself recoiling from legal positivism, and moving honestly (if temporarily) to reform its polities on the basis of ideas about human dignity and natural rights. Catholic philosophers and theologians like Jacques Maritain and John Courtney Murray did remarkable work trying to show how the Catholic tradition should seize the moment: notwithstanding the gentiles' disordered theories *about* the moral order, the experience of the war and its aftermath rendered them teachable.[32] In retrospect, we see that there was an overestimation, not only of what the gentiles knew, but also of what they were willing to do with their knowledge. (Perhaps the most bizarre overestimation of common ground came in 1989 with Cardinal Bernardin's recommendation that Catholic lawyers ought to adopt the natural law theory of Ronald Dworkin.[33]) From another point of view, we could say that there was a drastic underestimation of the Church's teaching mission. In the literature and discourse of that period, it is often difficult to say who was teaching whom.

Fifty years after World War II, in *Evangelium Vitae,* Pope John Paul II laments the fact that the children of Locke and Rousseau have decided to reject the natural law foundations of civil government. He writes:

A long historical process is reaching a turning-point. The process which once led to discovering the idea of "human rights"—rights inherent in every person and prior to any Constitution and State legislation—is today marked by a surprising contradiction. Precisely in an age when the inviolable rights of the person are solemnly proclaimed and the value of life is publicly affirmed, the very right to life is being denied or trampled upon, especially at the more significant moments of existence: the moment of birth and the moment of death.[34]

"[P]aradoxically," John Paul continues, what were once crimes now "assume the nature of 'rights,' to the point that the State is called upon to give them legal recognition." It is "sinister," the Pope says, that states are "departing from the basic principles of their Constitutions." For when they recognize as moral rights the rights to kill the weak and infirm, the "entire culture of human rights" is threatened. "It is a threat capable, in the end, of jeopardizing the very meaning of democratic coexistence."[35]

Thinking it had seized upon a moment favorable to making common cause with the modern notions of human dignity and rights, the Church finds that the culture has retreated from the few things that seemed right about its modernity. In any case, it is surely significant that most of the encyclical *Evangelium Vitae* involves a detailed exegesis of the first four chapters of Genesis. The Pope takes his audience back to the Scriptures. The gentiles need to be taught.

Piecemeal Theology

If the papacy overestimated the efficacy of the instruction *ad extra,* it underestimated the problems *ad intra.* Not only was natural law disembedded from moral theology, but moral theology was disembedded from the rest of theology. In his encyclical *Aeterni Patris* (1879), Leo XIII anticipated the problem of theology's being done piecemeal, with a lurching from issue to issue, and with the chief means of resolution being the application of authority. He wrote: "For in this, the most noble of studies, it is of the greatest necessity to bind together, as it were, in one body the many and various parts of the heavenly doctrines, that, each being allotted to its own proper place and derived from its own proper principles, the whole may join together in a complete union."

Unfortunately, this ideal was not successfully realized prior to Vatican II. Perhaps the best account of the dwindling estate of moral theology before the Council is the recent book by Servais Pinckaers, O.P., *The Sources of Christian Ethics.* Regarding the typical presentation of moral theology in the manuals used in seminaries, Pinckaers notes:

> Moral theology was divided into fundamental and particular sections. Fundamental moral theology included four chapters, covering human acts, laws, conscience, and sins. Particular moral theology, after a chapter on the theological virtues and their obligations, was generally divided according to the Ten Commandments, to which were added the precepts of the Church and certain canonical prescriptions. The sacraments were studied in the light of the obligations required for their administration.[36]

If, *ad extra,* doctrines of natural law were being used to produce conclusions to vexed moral issues among the gentiles, the opposite tendency prevailed *ad intra*. The task of moral theology was to lay out premises from reason and church authority for the purpose of directing the legal dimension of marital and sacramental actions. Not only in the seminaries but also in the universities, the thought of St. Thomas was accorded great respect; yet it was extracted from the *Summa Theologiae* in a way that favored the rationalistic elements of law. Almost everyone who teaches Thomas today would agree with Pinckaers that Thomas's thought was deeply misrepresented when the first seven questions of the so-called Treatise on Law (*S.t.* I-II, qq. 90-97) were isolated from the questions on beatitude and virtue, and ultimately from the questions on the Old Law and the New Law.

The subject of natural law was placed in the most unfortunate position of being organized around two extreme poles. On the one end, it represented the conclusions of church authority; on the other, it represented what every agent is supposed to know according to what is first in cognition. We have Cartesian minds somehow under church discipline.

The response was inevitable. In our time, there is a deep and ultimately irrational reaction against any depiction, much less any organizing, of the moral life in terms of law. We cannot here sort through all the species of this reaction in contemporary moral theology. Earlier we saw Cardinal Roy trying to construe "order laid down by God" in any way that might avoid the notion of a legal order. As we will see in due course, *Veritatis Splendor* tries to moderate this reaction against the notion of conduct regulated by law. Yet the NCCB's advertising of the encyclical exemplified the very sort of reaction that *Veritatis Splendor* tries to moderate: "It reverses pre–Vatican II legalism by speaking of the good and the bad rather than the forbidden and permitted, and by speaking about the invitation to live a moral life in God rather than the enforcing of laws or norms." This is precisely the simplistic attitude that the encyclical tries to overcome.

Natural Law as Individual Autonomy

Before moving to *Veritatis*, let us look at one particular reaction against law, the reaction that the encyclical takes the most pains to refute. I have said that once natural law was disembedded from moral theology, and moral theology from theology, the concept was pre-

cariously stranded between two poles of authority: a chain of command somehow terminating in the authority of the Church, and a
chain of propositions somehow terminating in the individual mind.
Rather than fundamentally reconsidering this picture, casuists and
confessors valiantly endeavored to relieve the burden of conscience.
So, in the case of *Humanae Vitae,* the conclusions of the natural law
deriving the official chain of command seemed (to many) to conflict
with what individual "reason" pronounced.

We should not be surprised that casuistry would not have the last
word. Natural law itself would have to be reformulated to side with
individual conscience. Through the sluice-gates of this problem, the
distinctively modern notions of natural law as individual autonomy
would flow into Catholic moral theology. If this response went no
further than to claim the individual's competence to respond to divine
providence (with the Church as a non-authoritative support), then
the story would have ended with a surprising "Protestant moment"
for Catholic moral theology. But that is not where it ended. At least
in contemporary moral theology, it ends with the claim of autonomy
in the face of providence: the creator God exists, perhaps, but he does
not govern.

For example, in his most recent book, Father Joseph Fuchs contends:

> When in fact, nature-creation does speak to us, it tells us only what
> it is and how it functions on its own. In other words, the Creator
> shows us what is divinely willed to exist, and how it functions, but
> not how the Creator wills the human being qua person to use this
> existing reality.[37]

Fuchs goes on to assert:

> Neither the Hebrew Bible nor the new Testament produces state-
> ments that are independent of culture and thus universal and valid
> for all time; nor can these statements be given by the church or its
> magisterium. Rather, it is the task of human beings—of the various
> persons who have been given the requisite intellectual capacity—
> to investigate what can and must count as a conviction about these
> responsibilities.[38]

In other words, God creates, but he gives no operating instructions.[39]

Father Fuchs further asserts: "One cannot . . . deduce, from God's relationship to creation, what the obligation of the human person is in these areas or in the realm of creation as a whole."[40] Regarding *Gaudium et Spes,* where the human conscience is spoken of as a *sacrarium* in which we find ourselves responsibly before God—*solus cum solo*[41]—Fuchs states that the notion that the human person "is illuminated by a light that comes, not from one's own reason . . . but from the wisdom of God in whom everything is created . . . cannot stand up to an objective analysis nor prove helpful in the vocabulary of Christian believers."[42]

Father Fuchs's rejection of the Council's teaching on the nature of conscience at least has the virtue of consistency. It follows from his own doctrine that while God creates, he does not govern the human mind. The human mind is a merely natural light, to which there corresponds a merely natural jurisdiction over ethics. In its work of discovering moral norms, the mind discovers the contextual proportions of good and evil, case by case as it were. Although Fuchs struggles to avoid the implication, it would seem that a general statute of positive law could never concretely bind human conscience, because it could never adequately measure the proportions of good and evil across cases and contexts. At best, law would be a summary of previous findings, which then functions as an indicator (rather than a norm) of present or future choices.

Hence, specifically on the issue of natural law, Fuchs insists that "[a] classical understanding of natural law is basically a 'positivist' understanding of natural law (a static law 'written on nature'), and precisely does not offer genuine natural law as the living and active creaturely participation in God's eternal wisdom."[43] The traditional words are still present: e.g., "written on the heart," "participation in God's eternal wisdom." But they now mean something different, and in fact the opposite of the tradition in Augustine and Aquinas. For the older tradition, there is a clear distinction between the mind's *discovering* or discerning a norm and the being or *cause* of the norm. The human mind can go on to make new rules because it is first ruled. This, in essence, is the doctrine of participation as applied to natural law. Natural law designates for Fuchs, however, the human power to make moral judgments, not any moral norm regulating that power— at least no norm extrinsic to the operations of the mind. This is not a subtle departure from the tradition; it is no more subtle than the difference between giving a teenager the keys to the car with a set of instructions, and just giving him the keys to the car.

"VERITATIS SPLENDOR": REAFFIRMING FOUNDATIONS

The encyclicals usually have pastoral purposes. Fundamental principles are cited only insofar as they are needed to address the problem at hand, or perhaps to remind the faithful of what every one believes. *Veritatis Splendor* takes a different approach. Noting that the Church has proposed moral teaching on "many different spheres of human life," Pope John Paul goes on to declare: "Today, however, it seems necessary to reflect on the *whole* of the Church's moral teaching, with the precise goal of recalling certain fundamental truths of Catholic doctrine which, in the present circumstances, risk being distorted or denied."[44]

Veritatis Splendor is not aimed at consensus-building among the gentiles. It is addressed to the episcopacy. And it is chiefly concerned not with applied ethics but with the foundations of moral theology.[45]

The first statement about the crisis over foundations concerns the authority of the Church: "The Magisterium itself is considered capable of intervening in matters of morality only in order to 'exhort consciences' and to 'propose values,' in the light of which each individual will independently make his or her decisions and life choices."[46]

If the crisis concerned only the authority of the Church, the Pope would be putting moral theology into precisely the corner where the modern mind wants it: for it would look like the assertion of a this-worldly power to command an assertion that is immediately answered by a counter-assertion of the authority of individual conscience. The Pope needs to show that being commanded by another is not merely a device of ecclesiastical powers and offices; it is not created by papal authority or by tradition.

The Pope therefore reformulates the issue:

[C]ertain moral theologians have introduced a sharp distinction, contrary to Catholic doctrine, between an "ethical order," which would be human in origin and of value for "this world" alone, and an "order of salvation" for which only certain intentions and interior attitudes regarding God and neighbor would be significant. This has then led to an actual denial that there exists, in Divine Revelation, a specific and determined moral content, universally valid and permanent. The word of God would be limited to proposing an exhortation . . . which the autonomous reason alone would then have the task of completing with normative directives which are truly "objective," that is, adapted to the concrete historical situation.[47]

Here, at last, we reach something fundamental for moral theology. Is the moral order a creature of divine providence, or does divine governance have to be added on to an already complete and autonomous human jurisdiction over morals? Here we are not worrying about the morality of gambling or contraception. Rather, the problem is the condition(s) of the possibility of moral theology. If God provides only the "natural" conditions for human practical reason, giving the human mind a kind of plenary authority over all the material norms, then God does not govern—except perhaps in the metaphorical fashion suggested by some of the deists. The Pope goes on to say:

Were this autonomy to imply a denial of the participation of the practical reason in the wisdom of the divine Creator and Lawgiver, or were it to suggest a freedom which creates moral norms, on the basis of historical contingencies or the diversity of societies and cultures, this sort of alleged autonomy would contradict the Church's teaching on the truth about man. It would be the death of true freedom: "But of the tree of the knowledge of good and evil you shall not eat, for in the day that you eat of it you shall die" (Gen 2:17).[48]

Throughout *Veritatis,* the Pope tries to give all three foci of natural law their due: (1) an order of nature (the "truth about man"), (2) the rudiments of which are "in principle accessible to human reason"[49] (3) and are expressions of divine providence. At least in passing, he notes the relevance of the first two of these to the "demands of dialogue and cooperation with non-Catholics and non-believers, especially in pluralistic societies."[50] Reflection on the good and evil of human acts and of the person who performs them is "accessible to all

---

peoples."[51] However, there can no mistaking the main emphasis of the encyclical, which concerns number three.

The Strategy: Dialogue With God

The question is how to give all three foci their due, while still showing their proper organization in theology. In the *Institutes,* John Calvin quotes St. Bernard of Clairvaux:

> With propriety, therefore, Bernard teaches that the gate of salvation is opened to us, when in the present day we receive the Gospel with our ears, as death was once admitted at the same doors when they lay open to Satan. For Adam had never dared to resist the authority of God, if he had not discredited his word.[52]

The Pope adopts a similar strategy of exposition, one that is dialogical from the very beginning. While never denying the fact that man enjoys natural starting points for grasping moral good and evil, the Pope puts man into conversation with God; he interrupts the soliloquy.

Notice how the major chapters of *Veritatis Splendor* are arranged:

- In the first, the reader is situated along the road where the rich young man encounters Christ (Matt. 19). The Pope contends that questions about the good are essentially religious questions.
- In the second, the reader is re-situated in the light of the original conversation between God and man in Genesis 2. Most of the discussion of natural law takes place in this context.
- In the third, the reader is turned toward the world, according to the theme of martyrdom and witness.
- In the conclusion, the reader stands with Mary at the foot of the cross.

The Pope explains in the first chapter that the first and ultimate question of morality is not a lawyerly question. Unlike the Pharisees, the rich young man does not ask what the bottom line is, from a legal standpoint. Rather, he asks what must be done in order to achieve the unconditional good, which is communion with God. Christ takes the sting out of law, not by annulling it, but by revealing the Good to which it directs us. Remove or forget the Good and law inevitably becomes legalism.

The Scripture relates that the young man went away sad, for he had many possessions. But the modern audience is more apt to turn away sad when faced with the teaching that there is a moral law that is indispensable, and that indeed binds authority itself. The Pope points out that all issues of circumstance, culture, place, and time notwithstanding, certain actions can never be made right; no human "law" can make them right. Just as from the scales and axiomatic measures of music there can come a Beethoven sonata or a Schoenberg twelve-tone composition, so obedience to the commandments opens the possibility of a creative, fluid, and completely realized human liberty. The point of learning the musical scales is not to engage in mindless repetition; the point is to prepare to make beautiful music. A piano teacher who taught only the scales would be a legalistic simpleton. But a piano teacher who *neglected* to teach these rudiments would be unworthy of the name teacher. Musical order cannot begin solely with human spontaneity and creative improvisation. And the same is true in the domain of moral action. Anyone who sets up an opposition between law and freedom, and then takes the side of freedom, not only underestimates the need for law but also misrepresents the nature of freedom.

The story of the rich young man shows the essential unity of the law and the Gospel, and in *Veritatis* the Pope spends considerable effort on a related theme: the unity of the two tables of the Decalogue. "Acknowledging the Lord as God," he says, "is the very core, the heart of the law, from which the particular precepts flow and toward which they are ordered."[53] Each precept, he continues, "is the interpretation of what the words 'I am the Lord your God' mean for man."[54]

"To ask about the good," in fact, "ultimately means to turn towards God," the fullness of goodness. Jesus shows that the young man's question is really a "religious question, and that the goodness that attracts and at the same time obliges man has its source in God, and indeed is God himself."[55] Georges Cottier, the Dominican theologian of the papal household, has underscored the importance of this point in the encyclical:

. . . awareness of the self as an image of God is at the root of moral judgements, beginning with the norms of the moral law. . . . The image is turned toward its Archetype and is the origin of a desire for union with it and assimilation to it. The natural law makes known to our reason the essential goods to which we must tend in order to reach God, who is the supreme Good.[56]

Back to Genesis

In the second chapter, the Pope takes the discussion of the foundations of the moral order back to the original situation in Genesis 2. This is the patristic common place for the discussion of natural law. Ever since his catechesis on Genesis, given during his weekly audiences in 1979-80 (published under the title "Original Unity of Man and Woman"), the Pope has returned over and over to the first four chapters of that book.[57]

Some people . . . disregarding the dependence of human reason on Divine Wisdom . . . have actually posited a "complete sovereignty of reason" in the domain of moral norms regarding the right ordering of life in this world. Such norms would constitute the boundaries for a merely "human" morality; they would be the expression of a law which man in an autonomous manner lays down for himself and which has its source exclusively in human reason. In no way could God be considered the Author of this law, except in the sense that human reason exercises its autonomy in setting down laws by virtue of a primordial and total mandate given to man by God. These trends of thought have led to a denial, in opposition to Sacred Scripture (cf. Mt 15:3-6) and the Church's constant teaching, of the fact that the natural moral law has God as its author, and that man, by the use of reason, participates in the eternal law, which it is not for him to establish.[58]

Turning to the injunction in Genesis 2:17, the Pope writes:

By forbidding man to "eat of the tree of the knowledge of good and evil," God makes it clear that man does not originally possess such "knowledge" as something properly his own, but only participates in it by the light of natural reason and of Divine Revelation, which manifest to him the requirements and promptings of eternal wisdom. Law must therefore be considered an expression of divine wisdom.[59]

The natural condition of man is one of participation in a higher norm. Man has liberty to direct himself because he is first directed by another.[60]

The Pope makes use of a number of authorities to express the idea of natural law as "participated theonomy."[61] He refers to Psalm 4:6, "Let the light of your face shine upon us, O Lord" emphasizing that moral knowledge derives from a divine illumination;[62] using Romans 2:14, "The Gentiles who had not the Law, did naturally the things of the Law," he calls attention to the idea that it is not just by positive law that humans are directed in the moral order;[63] from Gregory of Nyssa he cites the passage that autonomy is predicated only of a king;[64] and from St. Bonaventure he cites the dictum that conscience does not bind on its own authority but is rather the "herald of a king."[65] The very existence of conscience, the Pope argues, indicates that we are under a law that we did not impose upon ourselves.[66] Conscience is not a witness to a human power; it is a witness to the natural law. And this is only to say that the natural law is a real law that cannot be equated with our conscience. It was precisely this equation, the Pope notes, that beguiled our first parents, when the serpent in Genesis 3:5 said they could be as gods. What does it mean to be "as gods"? It means that the human mind is a measuring measure, having plenary authority to impart the measures of moral good and evil.

The Pope also notes that the topic of natural law has been too readily detached from the economy of divine laws and pedagogy:

> Even if moral-theological reflection usually distinguishes between the positive or revealed law of God and the natural law, and, within the economy of salvation, between the "old" and the "new" law, it must not be forgotten that these and other useful distinctions always refer to that law whose author is the one and the same God and which is always meant for man. The different ways in which God, acting in history, cares for the world and for mankind are not mutually exclusive; on the contrary, they support each other and intersect. They have their origin and goal in the eternal, wise and loving counsel whereby God predestines men and women "to be

conformed to the image of his Son" (Rom 8:29). God's plan poses
no threat to man's genuine freedom; on the contrary, the acceptance
of God's plan is the only way to affirm that freedom.[67]

No Cosmic Tenure for Moral Theologians

It is surely a token of the disrepair of Catholic moral theology that
the Bishop of Rome would have to remind the episcopacy, and
through them the moral theologians, that natural law does not constitute a sphere of immunity (a kind of cosmic tenure for moral
theologians) from the plan of divine laws.[68] But once again, what the
Pope has to grapple with in this respect is not only decades of neglect
ad intra, where the theme of natural law was detached from the fundamental principles of theology, but also the history *ad extra,* where
natural law and natural rights betokened that ground of liberty in
which men find themselves under no mundane authority. This secular
myth, which was developed as a counter to Genesis, is contrary to the
most fundamental principles of Christian theology.

However the Church might find a common ground of discourse
with the gentiles, it cannot be done on the basis of that counter myth.
Of course, some truths about the nature of man and the structure of
moral reasoning are, as the Pope says, "in principle accessible to
human reason." He does not discredit the effort of modern polities
to affirm human rights and to place moral limits upon the power of
the state.

Having duly noted the existence of principles proximate to human
reason, the Pope emphasizes two things that correspond to the two
foci of natural law that he says less about: natural law in the mind,
and natural law in nature. First, he reminds the reader of the wounded
human condition that needs to be repaired by Christ:

> What is more, within his errors and negative decisions, man
> glimpses the source of a deep rebellion, which leads him to reject
> the truth and the good in order to set himself up as an absolute
> principle unto himself: "you will be like God" (Gn 3:5). Con-
> sequently, freedom itself needs to be set free. It is Christ who sets
> it free: He "has set us free for freedom" (cf. Gal 5:1).[69]

Second, he insists that human reason, endeavoring to construct the conditions for human fulfillment, needs revelation and grace:

Only in the mystery of Christ's Redemption do we discover the "concrete" possibilities of man. It would be a very serious error to conclude . . . that the Church's teaching is essentially only an "ideal" which must then be adapted, proportioned, graduated to the so-called concrete possibilities of man, according to a "balancing of the goods in question." But what are the "concrete possibilities of man"? And of which man are we speaking? Of man dominated by lust or of man redeemed by Christ?[70]

SOME IMPLICATIONS FOR PROTESTANTS

What can evangelical Protestants learn from this story? They might conclude that Karl Barth was right in saying:

It [moral theology] is in agreement with every other ethics adduced to the extent that the latter is obviously aware—explicitly or implicitly—of its origin and basis in God's command; to the extent that it does not seek authorization before any other court; to the extent that it actually attests the existence and validity of this principle. But it cannot and will not take it seriously to the extent that it tries to deny or obscure its derivation from God's command, to set up independent principles in face of autonomies and heteronomies which comprise the theonomy of human existence and action, to confront divine ethics with a human view of the world and of life which is supposed to have its own (if anything) superior value, and to undertake the replacement of the command of the grace of God by a sovereign humanism or even barbarism.[71]

It would be tendentious, of course, to suggest a meeting of the minds between Barth and *Veritatis Splendor*. But on this one point of theonomous ethics, there is more than a merely facile similarity. By way of negation, we can agree that the modern, secular construction of natural law is contrary to the Gospel. It is as destructive within the house of Catholic moral theology as it was in the Protestant denominations, which passed through the challenge of deism and liberalism a century before the Catholic Church.

In a certain respect, the degrading of Catholic moral theology is more cruel because Catholicism has staked more on this issue of natural law than Protestantism. The repair will also be more complicated for Catholics, because, among other reasons, the Catholic tradition has regarded the foci of natural law in the mind and natural law in things as having at least some intelligibility for those who know little or nothing of the revelation of Jesus Christ, and who have not given any effort to reconnecting these two foci back to the architectonic perspective of divine providence. The two cannot be brushed away under the rubric of the "epistemology of sin," as some Protestants are wont to do. Moreover, the Catholic Church has endeavored to address problems of justice in the temporal order according to principles immediately proximate to it.

The problem, for Catholics, is how to do all this without *ad extra* creating the misleading impression that these proximate principles are the end of the story, and also without *ad intra* reducing its own moral theology to a habit of extroversion—to having a merely worldly opinion about disputed issues in the temporal order, which opinion is then configured to conform to the consensus (if any) among the gentiles.

Moral Discourse on Public Matters

Today, especially in the United States, evangelical Protestants find themselves reconsidering the issue of natural law. Their interest seems to be occasioned by two things. First, the political success of evangelical Protestantism has made it necessary to frame an appropriate language for addressing civil politics and law. Second, evangelicals find themselves in dialogue with Catholics, with whom they share many common interests in matters of culture and politics—interests that would seem amenable to natural law discussion. Even though it is true that many Protestants today are chiefly interested in the use of natural law *ad extra,* as a way to speak to the "world," the lesson they might learn from recent Catholic moral theology runs in the other direction. For assuming the legitimate and persistent need of the Christian churches to address worldly issues of justice and morality, it is easy to lose control of this discourse, so that natural law makes moral theology superfluous, and even impossible.

It seems to me that the expression "natural law" ought to be avoided whenever possible in the Christian address to the world about worldly things. I realize that this is practically impossible, but I shall give the reasons anyway.

Catholics, and most Protestants, will agree that there is a sphere of moral discourse about public matters that can be distinguished from sermonics and catechetics. The question is whether we should refer to the moral discourse in this sphere as "natural law." Of course, we believe it is the natural law that renders the gentiles amenable to the rudiments of moral discourse. In view of the traditional Catholic understanding of this matter (still put forth in the new Catechism of the Catholic Church),[72] we believe that what the gentiles know is an effect of divine pedagogy, whether the gentiles know that or not. Christians do not need to teach or to construct the first rudiments of the "natural law," for this much is not the effect of human pedagogy in the first place. God, not our discourse, constitutes human creatures as moral agents. The basis of moral order will not stand or fall on whether, or to what extent, we use the words "natural law."

The problem is not whether the gentiles are moral agents, but rather the meanings they assign to the rudiments they possess by virtue of the natural law. In modern times, the rudiments have been gathered into ideologies of natural law or natural rights that not only are false but are expressed in the form of a belligerent universalism. In our country, there is a long tradition of political rhetoric about natural rights. Sadly, today most uses of this rhetoric are degraded, signifying the expansion of individual liberty on terms that are either non-moral or contrary to the moral order. Even John Courtney Murray insisted that the rhetoric was historically rooted in ideologies of the Enlightenment that ought to be corrected by a true account. Indeed, Murray's account of the American consensus includes explicit theological propositions about the relationship between moral order and divine providence. If there were a widespread dissent from these propositions, the basis for a public philosophy would collapse.[73]

"Good" and "Bad" Natural Law

Father Murray would have been mortified, but perhaps not completely surprised, by the spectacle of that collapse in our times. In 1991, on the eve of the Senate hearings on the nomination of

Clarence Thomas to the Supreme Court, Senator Joseph Biden took the position that the Judiciary Committee should explore whether Judge Thomas held a "good" or "bad" theory of natural law. A bad theory of natural law, in Biden's view, would seek to expound a "code of behavior . . . suggesting that natural law dictates morality to us, instead of leaving matters to individual choice."[74] A good theory would support individual rights of immunity against morals legislation on matters of personal sexual conduct and abortion. The natural law teachings in recent papal encyclicals would therefore have to be regarded as "bad."

For public purposes, it is more prudent to ridicule than to argue with positions like Biden's. But the problem remains. Christians in search of a sphere of public moral discourse quickly realize that they no longer live in the age of Jefferson and Lincoln. The rhetoric of natural law is abundant in the moral discourse of the public sphere, to be sure; but it is terribly degraded. The most serious setbacks in our political and legal order have been done in the name of natural law, abortion rights being the most evident but by no means the only case in point. How then do Christians correct the ideologies in which natural law is ensconced without going on to discuss those very things that public discourse is supposed to avoid? How can they avoid the task of having actually to reconstitute the sphere of public moral discourse? *If* Christians wish to do so, I can see no alternative than to restore natural law rhetoric to its true and adequate premises. At the very least, we should return to the older American custom of speaking of "higher law." This usage, employed by Martin Luther King, indicates the more than human ground for the public moral order.

The Church Fathers referred to pagan learning as the gold of Egypt, which can be melted down from the idols. But the modern ideologies of natural law and natural rights are quite different. For the moderns took the theological notion of natural law and reshaped idols. If it is necessary to take public discourse as it stands and by the arts of dialectic and rhetoric to move it away from the idols, this task must be done very cautiously. When the Christian theologian plays with the modern rhetoric of natural law, he should know that he is playing with something more than fire. *Ad extra,* he is apt to underestimate the anti-theological meanings of modern natural law (essentially, man as a free agent without God), meanings that are easily reinforced if the rhetoric is not corrected; *ad intra,* he is liable to bring the idols back into the house of moral theology.

Both of these problems are addressed in recent encyclicals. To conclude, let us return to John Paul II's example. As I pointed out earlier, the Pope vigorously supports the modern experiment in constitutional democracy and human rights. But once he discerned that the rhetoric of natural rights was being used to justify killing the unborn and infirm, he took his readers in *Evangelium Vitae* back to the book of Genesis. The gentiles need and deserve the whole truth, even in order to preserve the rationality embedded in their own "secular" experiment. As for the use of natural law within moral theology, *Veritatis Splendor* reintegrates natural law into the dogmatic theology of revelation and Christology. It seems to me that these two encyclicals, one aimed *ad extra,* the other *ad intra,* get the problem of natural law situated just about right.

A Response

Carl E. Braaten

The perspective I bring to this conversation between Protestants and Catholics about natural law is that of the Lutheran tradition, which has had its own distinctive way of appropriating and transforming the Catholic natural law tradition, though not with a lot of success. Today, however, the Lutheran label doesn't mean much. Much of Lutheranism is entering the mainstream of liberal American Protestantism and is fast losing its distinctive marks of confessional identity. A minority movement within Lutheranism known as "evangelical catholic" is bent on reclaiming the original intent of Luther and the confessors at Augsburg, which was to reform the one holy catholic Church according to the Gospel, not to start anything remotely resembling a modern Protestant denomination. Luther's reforming thrust *(evangelische Ansatz)* tragically resulted in schism, breaking up the structural unity of the western Church. As evangelical catholics we believe that the only true expression of Luther's theological vision is the ecumenical path toward reclaiming the unity of the Church in continuity with the apostolic Gospel and catholic faith.

Natural law is a part of the Catholic tradition, a part that Luther retained, though not without transforming its place and meaning within the framework of his overall understanding of the Gospel. But natural law or any revised version of it has never played the same role in Lutheran theology as it has in Roman Catholic theology. This helps to explain why there is nothing in our Lutheran tradition that corresponds to the comprehensive body of social teachings, with varying

---

Carl E. Braaten, former professor of systematic theology at the Lutheran School of Theology, Chicago, is the executive director of the Center for Catholic and Evangelical Theology, Northfield, Minnesota.

31

degrees of binding authority, to be found within the Roman Catholic Church. Lutherans, like most other Protestants, are floundering in a culture of moral chaos with scarcely any substantial tradition of theological ethics to draw from. We have an authoritative confessional tradition regarding the doctrines of the Gospel *(doctrinae evangelii)* but none regarding moral issues. Many are happy about the absence of moral teaching, because it leaves them free to make up a new morality to accommodate current trends in science and secular ideologies. And that is exactly what is happening with regard to the most controversial debates within our church, on, for example, abortion, euthanasia, homosexual behavior, and the ordination of gays and lesbians.

Lutherans do produce social statements, to be sure; but compared to Catholic social teaching, they lack both a basis for argument from natural law and an appeal to the Church's teaching authority. We have no teaching authority and no substantive theological ethic, so pastors and lay people are easy targets of the *Zeitgeist*. The appeal to the Bible as the sole authority in matters of faith and morals has not worked and cannot work, apart from the hermeneutical function of church tradition and the Church's teaching authority. Although Protestant social statements draw together the seemingly most relevant biblical passages on any issue, the troublesome ones are easily dissolved in the acids of historical criticism, which can be used to relativize and even nullify biblical teachings by showing that they are tightly bound to the cultural situation of the time in which they were written and therefore have no universal applicability.

In this situation of moral confusion and ethical wobbliness, many of our people—pastors, laity, and theologians—have welcomed the magisterial ministry of Pope John Paul II in behalf of the whole Church. Drawing as he does on the Bible, the ancient creeds and councils of the Church, and the fathers and doctors of the great tradition, sources that they also would affirm as authoritative for their own ministries, the Pope fills a void that they keenly sense in their own denomination.

The Appeal of Natural Law

The effort to recover something of the natural law tradition is occurring in the face of a secularized culture in which both the theory and the rule of law are in deep crisis. The rise of the positivistic theory of law prepared the way for the abuse of law by the totalitarian state, which manipulated law as a mere function of absolute power. Prior to the triumph of positivism, the law was thought to be a means of justice administered by the state, not a tool of arbitrary power. With the collapse of theological or metaphysical foundations of justice, there was no other ground of support, no other source, no other criterion of validity for the law than the will of those who held the monopoly of force. The twentieth century has witnessed the unforgettable horror of the "lawlessness of law." Legal positivism stands defenseless, stripped of the traditional appeal to transcendent norms beyond positive law. In positivistic theory, justice is determined by what the law says, rather than the law's being determined by what justice requires.

The fear of normlessness and its nihilistic effects in public life has sparked a revival of interest in the classical notion of natural law. Churches feel a sense of responsibility for the process of law in social life. Even when they cannot agree with Catholic natural law theory and its magisterial application from case to case, they secretly admire a church that knows where it stands on the issues and seems never short of reasons to explain why.

Protestants thought they could count on Catholics to hold the fort. But now Russell Hittinger tells us "it ain't necessarily so" and relates the sad tale of "how the concept of natural law became a serious problem in modern Catholic moral theology." Hittinger reminds us that in the Fathers and in Thomas Aquinas, natural law was always tethered to theology; it was never seen as an autonomous realm that functioned independently of the eternal law in the mind of God. But in the modern period, natural law declared its independence from theology as well as from the teaching authority of the Church. Here is a key conclusion by Hittinger:

> Thus what began for the Christian theologians as a doctrine explaining how the human mind participates in a higher order of law is turned into its opposite. The natural law becomes "temporal," the temporal becomes "secular," and the secular becomes the sphere in which human agents enjoy immunity from any laws other than those they impose upon themselves.

The granite foundation of natural law in real theology has been surrendered in exchange for the quicksand of modern secular ideology.

Not God but man has become the measure of all things. That all this could happen in Catholic moral theology since Vatican II, in a Church that claimed dominical legitimation for the twin pillars of sacred tradition and official authority to bracket its moral discourse, makes it easier to explain the ethical debacle in Protestantism, which enjoyed the benefits of neither of these pillars.

Barth and Natural Law

Russell Hittinger comes close to siding with Karl Barth, for whom the whole idea of a "natural law" or a "natural theology" functions like a Trojan horse inside the walls of the Church, within its theology and ethics. Hittinger even says: "It seems to me that the expression 'natural law' ought to be avoided whenever possible in the Christian address to the world about worldly things." Barth would add, not only the expression but the matter itself *(die Sache selbst)* should be avoided. Why? Because in Barth's view there lurks a kind of latent deism in natural law theory. Its cradle is not biblical revelation but pagan metaphysics. The God behind the metaphysics of natural law is not the living God of the Bible. Natural law theory creates an autonomous locus of moral reflection completely separate from the revelation of God in Jesus Christ. It does not take sin seriously and is overly optimistic about the human condition.

Hittinger seems to agree that it has indeed worked out that way in modern Catholic moral theology, and cites Joseph Fuchs among others as evidence. But Hittinger, unlike Barth, believes that natural law can be baptized, and that it has been salvaged in principle in recent papal encyclicals by the reintegrating of natural law "into the dogmatic theology of revelation and Christology." He believes that two recent encyclicals, *Evangelium Vitae* and *Veritatis Splendor,* "get the problem of natural law situated just about right."

Hittinger's argument is not with Karl Barth but with his fellow Catholic moral theologians who have detached natural law "from the fundamental principles of theology," which is exactly what Protestant critics have charged all along. What would Karl Barth have to say about the latest papal encyclicals? I don't know. (There is a story about Barth and the pope: Barth was told that a reporter had asked the pope who in his estimation was the greatest theologian of the century. The pope answered, "Why, Karl Barth, of course," to which Barth supposedly replied, "So the pope is infallible after all.") But while I cannot speak for Karl Barth, I myself agree with Hittinger's conclusion that to be useful in Christian moral teaching, natural law must be returned to its theological base, where, he claims, Thomas Aquinas firmly placed it. Hittinger is in good company in rescuing Thomas from Thomism, the kind of Thomism that separates what Thomas wrote about principles of law, reason, and nature from the wider framework of the Gospel, revelation, and the Church. For Thomas, what is first in the order of knowledge *(ordo cognoscendi)* is not necessarily first in the order of being *(ordo essendi)*. It is no mere coincidence that the misuse of natural law and natural theology in Catholic theology is concomitant with a longstanding misinterpretation of Thomas Aquinas.

The Orders of Creation

Just as a basic disagreement appears on the use of natural law in Catholic moral theology, so also there exists a disagreement of a different sort in Protestant theology. This surfaced in a heated way between Karl Barth's *koinonia* ethics and the Lutheran theology of the "orders of creation." The orders of creation *(Schoepfungsordnungen)* doctrine is the new baptismal name given to natural law by Lutheran theologians of the Erlangen school. The expression *lex creationis* takes the place of *lex naturae*. What is the difference? The change is intended to transpose the entire discussion of human life in the earthly city from the "unbaptized God" (to use Robert Jenson's term) of Hellenistic metaphysics to the living God of the Bible, "Maker of heaven and earth"—that is, from philosophy to the theology of the first article of the creed.

Orders of creation and natural law do have something in common: both affirm that Christians, like all other human beings, exist in a framework of universal structures that are there prior to and apart from the fact that Christians believe in Christ and belong to his Church. The first article of the creed comes before the second and third for a good reason. God has placed all human beings in particular structures of existence that are common to all, such as sexuality, family, community, work, and government. However, it is important to stress that these universal structures are not autonomous entities that run, as the deists thought, with a mind of their own. The law and commandments of the living God are revealed through these common structures of human existence, but this original and universal revelation is different from the special revelation of God in the history and gospel of Jesus Christ.

This means that there is a double revelation of God, and here lies my chief point of disagreement with the covenant theology of Karl Barth. For Barth there is only one revelation of God. There is only one Word of God, from which all structures, orders, commandments, and ethical norms for Christian living in the world must be derived. I do not agree with this approach. It empties the world of its meaning as a realm of divine providence and human involvement that goes on apart from knowledge of the Bible and outside the walls of the Church. People do not need to know Jesus Christ and accept his work of salvation to have some knowledge of what is right and good through the law of creation and through conscience, for God's "eternal power and divine nature . . . have been understood and seen through the things he has made" (Rom. 1:20).

Barth's attack on both Catholic natural law theory and the Lutheran theology of the orders of creation was so vehement that after World War II many Protestant theologians slid down the slippery slope of situation ethics. Theological ethics based on the orders of creation was aborted, and nothing arose to take its place. For a number of theological reasons Lutherans could not accept Barth's method of treating ethics, but after the war they could not come together on an alternative. Moreover, Barth now had the advantage of standing on high moral ground as the author of the Barmen Declaration. Anyone who attacked the Barmen Declaration for its faulty theology, its mono-Christological view of revelation, and its Christocratic view of the structures of common human existence would be accused of the "German Christian" heresy, of being a Nazi.

There is a connection between Barth's attack on natural theology and the "death of God" movement, as well as between his attack on natural law or the orders of creation and the parallel deconstruction of ontology, ethical norms, nomological principles, and traditional values. The churches have not yet recovered from the evacuation of serious moral discourse, from a free fall into antinomianism. Hittinger shows that antinomianism is the fate of natural law theory divorced from theology, but the same fate awaits a theology that cannot muster a defense against the moral relativism of situation ethics. Our churches are mired in the amoral marshland of antinomianism.

Distinguishing Law and Gospel

In his commentary on *Veritatis Splendor* Hittinger speaks of "the essential unity of the law and the Gospel." The unity lies in God, and therefore the law as well as the Gospel is the province of theology proper. It is also salutary to observe the distinction. Luther taught that theology is the fine art of drawing the proper distinction between law and Gospel, neither separating nor equating them. Law and Gospel are two different modes of God's activity in the world. But law comes before Gospel in the history of salvation and in human experience. In Genesis 1-11 Israel wrote a preamble to her covenant history, involving the whole human race, placing Adam before Abraham and Noah before Moses—which is to say that the living God was at work among the nations of the world prior to the election of Israel. Similarly, today God acts in all realms of life without any necessary contact with the preaching of the Gospel. Law is the instrument of God's activity, both the unwritten law in the structure of things and the written codes of law that seek to embody principles of justice. Law is universal and inescapable. It provides the mesh and matrix of life, embracing all persons, communities, and nations in their actual empirical existence, creating a degree of order in spite of the destructive consequences of sin.

Atheists and agnostics and humanists somehow know the law of the hidden God *(deus absconditus)* without believing in the God who has revealed himself in Jesus Christ. There is no salvation in this knowledge, but without it life would come to a halt. There would be nothing to be saved. Law is not an autonomous structure of worldly life. A Christian understanding of law must be grounded in theology, because it is the living God who is active, often anonymously, through the law that is operative in the world. God's activity is not dependent on or limited by human awareness and knowledge. God carries out his purposes in the world through leaders, events, and institutions, whether they know it or not; there is no sphere of life where he is not active through the law to promote his will. Natural law theory divorced from theology is the bad kind of natural law, because it does not reckon with the continuing presence and pressure of the living God through concrete demands that impinge inescapably on all human beings. In Luther's language this is the work of the left hand of God.

But then there is the work of the right hand of God. This is carried on through the election of Israel, through the life, death, and resurrection of Christ, and through the Church's ministry of preaching the Gospel and administering the sacraments, which mediate the divine promise of eternal life, hope, and salvation. The real casualty of the eclipse of law is the preaching of the Gospel. The law is the fundamental presupposition of the Gospel. The Gospel is not the word of God apart from the law. Each has a different function. The law of God meets every person somehow through the natural orders of life in history and society, and through the medium of conscience. The law is God's controversy with his creatures. The law is the power of negativity, in that it can terrify, accuse, condemn, punish, and kill. If this is not true, then the Gospel cannot comfort, strengthen, forgive, liberate, and renew. Thus there are two uses of the law: the political use within the public domain, to order society, to prevent chaos, and to punish crime, and the religious use, which accuses and drives toward the Gospel (lex semper accusat). The Gospel is the medicine for the condition the law diagnoses. The law has no power to heal of itself.

Antinomianism in the pulpit turns the Gospel into a sweet anodyne that lulls people to sleep, when they should be roused by the law. The twofold process of demythologizing and psychologizing has removed the negative symbols of the biblical worldview—sin, Satan, the wrath of God, the final judgment, and hell. H. Richard Niebuhr captured it well in his characterization of the preaching of liberal Protestantism: "A God without wrath brought men without sin into a kingdom without judgment through the ministrations of a Christ without a cross."

Through the law God tells us what we must do; the Gospel declares what God does. The law is expressed in the imperative mood, the Gospel in the indicative. The law demands and threatens; the Gospel gives and forgives. The law says you ought to be righteous. It is reasonable to assume, said Kant, that if you ought to you can. That was the reasoning of Pelagius against Augustine and of Erasmus against Luther. The natural man is a born Pelagian. He hears the law and uses it as an occasion of pride and self-righteousness. But the law does more: it drives the self-reliant person into despair. It pulls the props from under a person and casts him or her into a slough of despondency, self-accusation, anxiety, and suicide. Thus the law prepares the way for the hearing of the good news of divine grace freely offered.

A Discarnate Logos

Russell Hittinger has told the story of how natural law has been misused, not only how it was "disembedded from moral theology," but how "moral theology was disembedded from the rest of theology." Yet to my mind this is only half the story. The other half concerns the *inner sanctum* of Christian theology, the Gospel of salvation on account of Christ alone. Karl Rahner was a dominant influence behind the scenes at Vatican II, and since then a kind of left-wing interpretation of Rahner's *logos* Christology has spread in the shape of a pluralistic theology of religions. Paul Knitter and other Catholic theologians have joined a parade of liberal Protestant theologians in affirming that Christ is a way of salvation, to be sure, but only for Christians; other religions have their own ways, equally valid and true. This pulls the plug on the universal mission of the Gospel to the nations.

In control of this pluralistic theology is the unbaptized *logos* of Greek metaphysics, the *logos asarkos,* which replaces the *logos* that became flesh in Jesus in a unique, definitive, and normative way. The mission of the Church has been radically redefined by the same sort of Catholic theology that secularizes natural law, only now it is the "scandal and stumbling block" of the Gospel itself that is demythologized.

The outcome of this idea of a discarnate *logos* salvifically at work in all the religions is that the missionary aim of the Church is no longer to bring the gentiles something they do not have, a gift of salvation. The Great Commission of Christ to his apostles and to all communities of faith that claim apostolic succession is effectually denied. The purpose of the Christian mission instead is to help Muslims be better Muslims, Hindus better Hindus, humanists better humanists, through dialogue and cross-fertilization of ideas. These pluralists believe it is more interesting and important to communicate their ideas about religion than to preach the Gospel to people of other religions. Preaching the Gospel might bring about conversion; to attempt that would be arrogant, triumphalistic, colonialistic. They call their theory of religions a Copernican revolution. It is no such thing; it is plain old-fashioned heresy popularized by liberal Protestantism.

Russell Hittinger has shared with us an eloquent lamentation about the collapse of natural law in modern Catholic moral theology. Equally sad, at least for me, is to see how Catholic theologians have followed the liberal Protestant theologians, Ernst Troeltsch and company, in reaming out the Christological core of the Christian faith so that there is no Gospel left to tell to the nations. The Pope's encyclical *Missio Redemptoris* was right on target in taking aim at and hitting this pluralistic theology of religions and the new missiology that follows from it.

I believe that the underlying cause of the problem of a secularized natural law, and of the notion of salvation in non-Christian religions apart from Christ, is a theological method that approaches issues from a philosophical concept of the *logos* outside the framework of a Christocentric, trinitarian monotheism. This is the unbaptized *logos* of pagan philosophy that the Church Fathers transformed—but perhaps not radically enough—under the conditions of their belief in the incarnation of the *logos* in the concrete person of Jesus of Nazareth, the *logos* made flesh.

Comments

Russell Hittinger: What Barth had to say about modern liberal theology strikes me as pretty accurate. But I do think that the problem here is not just natural law, because you could pick up other themes in theology and find the same thing—a loss of theological perspective altogether. The missionary aim of the Church seems to have been lost, at least among Catholic moral theologians, since World War II. Quite likely, the cause of this loss dates largely from before that. Certainly after World War II it seems that man-without-God is treated as an ontological fact; it is one thing to observe that many people do not know God, but it is quite another thing to posit man-without-God as a normative fact for Catholic moral discourse. My quotation of Cardinal Roy and his "modern synonyms" is typical of the period. So at this point the Church seems to have no teaching mission.

Rarely does Catholic natural law theory today seek to teach the reader what natural law is in terms of all three foci—human mind, nature, mind of God. Almost always it's simply a matter of taking what people already know and trying either to clarify it logically or apply it to issues of public policy. The divine origin and end of natural law is discarded, perhaps because it is a stumbling block to political consensus. This is not just a neglect of natural law—it's the abandonment of the mission of teaching unbelievers something they don't already know.

Carl Henry: Russell Hittinger and Carl Braaten have given us a fine beginning. But what is this natural law that is in debate? I went to Loyola for a course on Thomas and a course on Scotus. I went to

---

Note: The participants in this conversation are identified on pages 173-74.

Indiana University and took a course with Henry Veatch, who later taught at Georgetown as well, specially on natural theology and Thomas's fivefold proof of the existence of God. Never was it questioned that Thomas *believed* in the self-revealing God. The issue seemed to be, rather, a specific philosophical formulation. Without any appeal to divine revelation, but simply on the basis of observation, one assertedly could give a logical demonstration of the existence of God and of the existence and immortality of the soul.

Now I'm told that this misrepresents Thomas. What I'd like to know is, precisely what is the natural law? Let's define it as closely as we can. I'm willing to learn.

Russell Hittinger: My paper claims that you cannot define natural law except through the third of the three foci: order in the mind of God. Natural law as real law is not order in the human mind; to define it that way would be to make a terrible semantic and ultimately metaphysical mistake. The pagans didn't have a doctrine of natural law, but they did have a concept of justice according to nature, conformity of the mind to what was the naturally just or honest thing.

Christian theologians upgrade this quite considerably, and that creates part of the problem. Christians talk about *lex*. From Tertullian onwards, natural law is defined as God's governance of the creature through indited, impressed law. Creatures are moved, even prior to their practical reason, to reason practically in a certain way, and that's called law. There's a legislator, there's an end, and there's a promulgation. Thomas never thought, however, that the creature being moved by the order of creation, or by the eternal law, must immediately *know* that he or she is being so moved. One of the ways in which natural law differs from positive law is that the creature is moved by God, sweetly—as said in Wis. 8:1, *suaviter*—through his own nature.

Carl Henry: Is there a body of universally shared moral knowledge that is conveyed through natural law?

Russell Hittinger: I think one overstates the case to say that anything but the rudiments of moral law are known *naturaliter*. According to Aquinas, one of the prices paid for sin is that the mind is separated from knowing God and therefore is governed by God only through these effects. For us to cooperate with that divine governance and to develop a body of law that is congruent with it is very difficult without divine instruction known through Scripture and tradition.

Robert Royal: Just to clarify, because Carl Henry and I have discussed this point at other Ethics and Public Policy Center functions: In the *Summa* it says *quinque viae*—five *ways*—by which we approach the divine. Aquinas gives the impression that these are proofs. But would it be fair to say that they are *approaches* rather than proofs?

Russell Hittinger: Thomas certainly felt in principle that the existence of God could be demonstrated. But for Aquinas, most people know without demonstration that God exists. In *Summa Contra Gentiles* he says that you can infer but not necessarily demonstrate the existence of God from things that are seen. People who don't, he says, are guilty of plain stupidity. Natural reason, however, cannot know of special providence and that God is Trinity.

Carl Braaten: Well, I don't use the term "natural law." As I said in my paper, in the Lutheran tradition the concept is taken up into the first article of the creed, which does what you're saying must be done, namely, locate natural law within theology. Whatever term you're using, natural law or orders of creation, it refers to God's ordering of human life. God does this through some enduring structures, and that's the *humanum*—you could say human nature, or the imprint of God on the human being through creation. The human being is a social being, so that there are certain givens, certain common human structures of life and experience. It's possible for us to go to China and have a conversation with people from a totally different religious, cultural, and language background. There has to be some kind of common precondition for the possibility of human discourse. The epistemological question, "How do we know?," is another issue. But theology must affirm that before redemption there is a human being, fallen and sinful though he may be; there is a universal human condition that is the presupposition of the entire history of salvation.

When I went to Japan a missionary said, "How can we preach the Gospel here in Japan, since the people have no sense of sin? They have a sense of shame, but no sense of sin." But the Japanese are human beings for whom Christ died and for whom he was raised from the dead. There is a common human predicament. I think theology has something at stake in this whole discussion. We don't have to produce a definition once for all time, but we can keep working at it.

Carl Henry: I don't question that man comes into life epistemically loaded with certain baggage through the *imago Dei* and the whole structuring of the human situation with its transcendent roots in God's creation and revelation. None of that do I question. What I'm asking is whether natural law has a specific moral content that is universally shared, a body of truth that somehow survives the Fall and is universally shared. If not, then what I learned about even Thomas's view of natural law was not an accurate representation.

Robert George: I would like a crack at Dr. Henry's question. I think the natural law is a body of practical—including moral—principles that provide reasons, more than merely instrumental reasons, for action and for restraint. The natural law, then, is how God directs man, made in God's image and likeness and, as such, endowed with reason and freedom, toward his proper ends. Non-human animals God directs in a different way. Man, made in his image, with reason and freedom, is directed by God through the natural law. In that way, it seems to me, the natural law is a participation in the eternal law, as the natural law theorists say. Or, the natural law is the moral law or God's law insofar as it is available to unaided reason. I agree with Carl Braaten that *how we know* the reasons, including moral reasons, that taken together constitute the body of the natural law is another question. Those of us who believe there are such reasons can debate the epistemological and cognitional questions. But the common ground, it seems to me, is the belief that there are such reasons and that they do constitute a body.

Are they shared? Yes and no. Shared, yes, in the sense that in principle these reasons are available to all of us as possessors of a practical intellect that can grasp those reasons. But shared in that everyone knows all of them perfectly or that we all agree, or could in this vale of tears agree, on them? No, because reason and inference can miscarry in the practical sphere, as they can in any other domain of inquiry, from mathematics to the sciences to historiography to logic itself. So it's true that we have broad differences over moral questions, and even over some practical questions that we wouldn't want to define as moral questions. But those differences themselves are no evidence at all for the proposition that no natural law exists.

I take Dr. Henry's question to be a request not for a definition but rather for an account of the natural law. Is it a body of principles? Yes. Are these principles "shared"? Yes, in one important way; but no, in another.

Daniel Westberg: The point has been made, but I think it's worth repeating, that the principles are not necessarily the equipment of every human mind. If we say we can appeal to people's natural knowledge, then people will falsify the theory of natural law by saying, "I don't accept that." The Thomistic view of natural law is that the principles are accessible; that doesn't mean that people have availed themselves of them. That's an important point.

James Schall: In revelation, as I understand it, there is a command that we believe that God exists. There are also certain indications that the existence of God could be shown in some fashion. It seems to me that what used to be called the preambles to the faith meant precisely that we have to have some grounding by which any revelation is credible to us. That credibility cannot itself, in my view, be revelation. We need some grounding for our ability to say that what is available to us by revelation is, in fact, not irrational. And so I think it is crucial that we defend the integrity of the intellectual experience as a set of questions that prepare us to receive the answers as given by faith.

David Smolin: I think there is a very serious Reformed/Catholic split there. The way I understand the Reformed faith, the only reason to accept revelation is God himself.

Russell Hittinger: Thomas would agree with you on that. Faith, if it is simply an epistemic exercise of believing something unseen, is not a theological virtue for St. Thomas. Anyone can have it. "Did you hear that the Cardinals won yesterday?" I didn't see it but I believe it. The virtue of faith is believing precisely on the authority of the

God who reveals himself. You were right on that point: there is no other way into that one but through the Holy Ghost, moving the heart that moves the mind to assent. That's Thomism 101. I think it may be Christianity 101.

James Skillen: Russ, after you've quoted Fuchs, you say in your paper, "The traditional words are still present, e.g., 'written on the heart' . . . but they now mean something different, and in fact the opposite of the tradition in Augustine and Aquinas. For the older tradition, there is a clear distinction between the agency of the mind *discovering* or discerning a norm and the being or *cause* of the norm." Part of what I want to get at is the distinction between the norm itself and the response. Hasn't a big ambiguity been present, ever since the Fathers began to absorb Aristotle or the Stoics or whatever, as to what this relation is?

For example, the first of the three foci you mentioned was natural law in the human mind. In this regard, it seems to me that quite often the discussion goes, does "in the human mind" mean being part of the subject? In a certain sense could one say that natural law means that the human being unavoidably reaches certain conclusions, because the structure of the mind is such that the mind is the law for itself? Part of what I'm getting at is that you see an antithesis between modern relativistic or antinomian . . .

Russell Hittinger: Well, no, because Kant is not a relativist or an antinomian, but he's the antithesis of what I'm trying to say about the Catholic tradition.

James Skillen: We're now saying that what most Catholics and Protestants mean by natural law and natural rights is the opposite of what the Christian tradition was saying by affirming that the mind is bound by a higher authority, by a law outside itself. How did we get to that situation? It seems to me that the whole movement toward the autonomous person grows out of the sense of being a law to myself. At a certain point in history humanism built up quite a head of steam in saying, "Neither God nor master! We'll be masters of ourselves." A pretty simple reply to that would be to say, "You're going to have to get back to God to be able to make sense out of life in this world."

That gets pretty close to a Barthian approach of saying, "Look, without God's grace breaking in to call people back in repentance to the proper will, there is no discerning of the law or being in tune with it." That in no way denies the validity of the continuing relevance of the law as binding on the person's conscience, but it certainly says that those who refuse to yield to it are out to lunch.

There's a kind of latent pantheism in some of the ancient thought that the Fathers picked up. If the mind of the person is that which is God in him, if there is such a close identity of the mind with what is divine, then you eventually get to the modern theme that we are God. Couldn't one of the tracks by which we try to correct this be to clarify how the meaning of divine law, divine normativity, creation order, whatever you want to call that complex of what the Creator puts to his creature, is always above and beyond them, never to be found in the mind? All we can say is that human beings, as we live in God's world, never escape the binding power of the law.

I'm trying to force apart this idea that somehow the law on the one hand is identified with the very subject itself and on the other hand is the norm beyond that subject. At that point we can also begin to make sense out of why it's so difficult to talk about natural law, when Protestant common grace doctrine and Catholic natural law doctrine were supposed to give us the common ground on which we could finally meet, all of us, simply as rational creatures.

Russell Hittinger: These words are very tricky, especially if you go through the three foci of natural law. For instance, the noun in its nominative case—*natura*—is not the best one theologically. The adverb—*naturaliter*—works better. It's not merely coincidental that the Church Fathers and even Aquinas used the adverb wherever possible to avoid the suggestion that nature *is* a law. They weren't stupid. They knew you can't just predicate a law of nature, except in the metaphorical sense. But nature can be a mode of promulgation by a divine legislator.

In modern terms, the fact that something is internal would mean that it is part of the very essence of the thing it is internal to. Aquinas has long discussions of this issue; in short, natural law is psychologically internal but metaphysically extrinsic to the person. So, for instance, desire is internal, but the final cause isn't.

By analogy, for Thomas, the natural law, insofar as it's real law, is an extrinsic principle. By the way, Thomas mentions three extrinsic principles of action: *diabolus, lex, gratia*—the devil, law, and grace. The natural law is extrinsic, but not external; whereas positive law is extrinsic and almost always external. Aquinas makes that distinction in his commentary on Aristotle's *Metaphysics,* but almost no one ever talks about it. It is crucial in Aquinas to sort out what these words mean so that you don't get lost in them. Because indeed, when you use nature in the nominative case, it can look as though you are predicating a law of nature. At that point you're in big trouble theologically. You may not be in big trouble epistemologically—just as you can go on counting while having an absolutely terrible theory of mathematics, I suppose. You can go on reasoning about this body of law while having a terrible theory about it. I would predict, though, that you won't go on reasoning well for very long. At a certain point the mind is going to want another reflective account of what it's doing. If we should start thinking of nature or the human mind as the law, we are in big trouble.

James Skillen: I still wonder how, if Aquinas is as clear as we think he is (I'm not trying to load this on Aquinas; I'm really talking about the whole tradition of Christianity, including the dilemma of the Reformers and modern liberal Protestants as well), if natural law puts us in such a position that we should have the ability to make these distinctions, at least within the framework of the Christian world, how can we have gotten to the point where it's so difficult to get agreement on what natural law means?

Russell Hittinger: But this happens all the time; it's not just natural law theory. You know something without immediate reliance on theories about it.

James Skillen: In the political world where I am right now, if, for example, you raise the question, "Shouldn't a congressman be concerned to do justice, rather than simply satisfying people so he can get elected?" the typical response today is, "Well, who can know what justice is? That's something for scholars." How can there be so little agreement on such fundamental matters?

Russell Hittinger: Because the human mind naturally wants something more than just flat-footed cognition. The human mind wants to know the reasons also. If it doesn't look for these in the clear light of theory, it's going to get into the dim corners of ideology. We don't need theology to explain how people know that murder is wrong. That's the point I make at the end of my paper. If someone says, "You need theology to know that," then we are really in different worlds. You need a theology to *explain,* maybe, but not to know, the rudiments of natural law. I am an old-fashioned natural law theorist in the sense that I believe that God is the cause of the natural law. Human minds are a proximate cause of the *knowing* of it; but God is the cause *of the law*.

Deal Hudson: What people want natural law to be is a body of axioms about morality. Carl Braaten's response reminded me of how in 1974 I went to Princeton Seminary as a Protestant and came out wanting to be Catholic. What we're arguing about here is precisely the thing in the Catholic tradition that is so attractive and draws so many into the Catholic Church. The concept of natural law was the fuel for much Protestant reflection until Catholics decided that it was more like a Cartesian window on the universe than a way of being instructed by God through his creation.

Clearly, Carl Braaten wants Catholics to represent the traditional account of natural law because he thinks there is something in it that is very important for public life, something that has been lost. But, even apart from the theoretical problems, the whole epistemological problem caused by the Fall, caused by sin, may still subvert this more traditional account of natural law.

2

Calvin's Use of Natural Law

Susan E. Schreiner

An observation made by Arthur C. Cochrane three decades ago has proved correct: "The problem of natural law, at least in Calvin, will not die down."[1] In fact, natural law has been a hotly disputed topic in Calvin studies since the beginning of this century. In 1909, August Lang argued that Calvin found no place for natural law in his theological system and that natural law played no part in his judgment of legal and social conditions.[2] Lang was immediately contradicted by Gisbert Beyerhaus in his analysis of Calvin's view of the state. If Lang had studied Calvin's commentaries, insisted Beyerhaus, he would not have argued that Calvin was "no friend of natural law."[3]

Beyerhaus was supported by Ernst Troeltsch, who could not understand how "in face of his own quotations Lang can say that Calvin found no place for natural law in his system."[4] Troeltsch argued that natural law was simply a natural presupposition that permeated Calvin's thinking. According to Troeltsch, Calvin identified natural law with the Decalogue and thereby embodied "political and business knowledge, domestic and economic ethics in the ethics of Christianity, uniting the Old and New Testaments with Aristotle and Cicero and

---

Susan E. Schreiner is an associate professor of church history and theology at the University of Chicago Divinity School. She is the author of *The Theater of His Glory: John Calvin and the Natural Order* (Labyrinth Press; reprinted by Baker Book House, 1995).

51

deducing from the Decalogue an all-embracing ethics of the inner life which can only be inspired with the Christian spirit."[5] Troeltsch elaborated on this point by saying that Calvin held to the "old rationalistic interpretation of natural law," thereby creating an inner contradiction in his entire theology. On the one hand, Calvin recognized the rationalism of the *lex naturae,* and on the other, he asserted the "irrational character of the divine will."[6]

Émile Doumergue could not agree with either Lang or Troeltsch. Doumergue demonstrated that Calvin repeatedly spoke of the order of nature that gave rise to the law of nature. Moreover, he explained that natural law played both a positive and a negative role in Calvin's thought. While Calvin did not establish a juridical system of natural rights, he did affirm that there was a divinely willed order and law of nature. On the basis of this order of nature and natural law, Calvin discussed the "horizontal" legal or moral relations among men. But Doumergue cautioned that Calvin never admitted a law or morality independent from God.[7]

In 1934 Josef Bohatec took up the challenge of analyzing the place of natural law in Calvin's theology. He criticized previous studies for failing to provide "a description of nature as the source and origin of natural law, as well as the psychological and ethical presuppositions of natural right." Bohatec called for a historical investigation and a discussion of how the doctrine of natural law functioned in a synthetic relationship with Calvin's other ideas.[8]

The Barth-Brunner Controversy

However, Bohatec's call for a decisive historical analysis was not the primary influence on the future of scholarship regarding Calvin and natural law. In the same year that Bohatec published *Calvin und das Recht,* the controversy between Brunner and Barth broke out.[9] This theological debate pressed the question of whether Calvin taught the possibility of a natural knowledge of God's will by means of a natural law. The issue of natural law was placed with the larger epistemological question: can the fallen human being have a natural knowledge of God? As Cochrane and others have pointed out, this question was urgent because it involved the "very existence of the Evangelical church in Germany in its struggle against 'German Christians' who were affirming a natural knowledge of God and His will in German blood, race, soil, and history."[10]

Brunner argued that for Calvin "nature" is both a "concept of being and a concept of norm." When Calvin wrote that "nature teaches" or that "nature dictates," he was saying that God teaches.[11] According to Brunner, these phrases meant that the will of God was implanted in creation so that the concept of the *lex naturae* and the "order of nature" meant the same thing: "The will of God, imprinted upon all existence, implanted in it from creation, can therefore be recognized as such."[12] In Brunner's interpretation, "the theological importance of the concept of nature is shown by the fact that God can be known from nature. And this is not a confused knowledge, which can hardly be of interest to the Christian who knows the Word of God. . . . it is something highly important and necessary for the Christian as well. God demands of us that we know and honor him in his works."[13] In Brunner's analysis, the concepts of conscience, reason, the image of God, and sin all must be taken into account before one understands the Reformer's view of natural law.

> Even fallen man still has—thanks to the "portion" of the *imago* that he has retained—an immortal soul, a conscience in which the law of God is indelibly and irremovably implanted. But he also has an inclination towards truth and a capacity for recognizing truth [because] the *imago* which man retains is the principle of the *theologia naturalis* in the subjective sense, i.e., of that knowledge of God derived from nature, of which man is capable apart from revelation in Scriptures or in Jesus Christ.[14]

Karl Barth vehemently rejected Brunner's contention that Calvin's statements about a twofold knowledge of God (in creation and in Christ) could be used to support a natural theology. The natural knowledge of God from creation is "a possibility in principle but not a possibility in fact."[15] Sin has obliterated any possibility of a natural theology: "Between what is possible in principle and what is possible in fact there inexorably lies the fall."[16] Calvin used Romans 1:20 to demonstrate only that human beings are without excuse. God is revealed in all of his creation, but this testimony only renders us more guilty. For Barth, there could never be a "second, independent kind of knowledge . . . as if our reason, once it had been illumined, had of itself gained the power of sight."[17]

Calvin scholars lined up to take sides in this debate. Günter Gloede sided with his teacher, Emil Brunner.[18] Peter Brunner, Peter Barth, Wilhelm Niesel, and T. F. Torrance supported Barth.[19] In 1952, with the publication of Edward Dowey's book *The Knowledge of God in Calvin's Theology,* the controversy was renewed. Dowey upheld Brunner's general principles against the Barthian denial of any natural theology.[20] The same year brought T. H. L. Parker's *Calvin's Doctrine of the Knowledge of God.* Agreeing with Barth, Parker argued for the centrality of Christology and revelation in Calvin's theology over and against any concept of natural theology.[21]

Subsequently, several efforts were made to investigate the topic further. Arthur C. Cochrane denied Brunner's position that Calvin taught a knowledge of God's will "through a natural law implanted in all men from creation." Nonetheless, Cochrane recognized that Calvin's treatises were full of references to the conscience, the *imago Dei,* and the law of nature. He concluded, like Doumergue before him, that Calvin used natural law in both a positive and a negative sense.[22] In 1968 David Little argued for a limited theory of natural law on the basis of Calvin's theology. He contended that Calvin "believed that within the limits of general social and political reflection, human nature and reason dictate a few unexceptionable moral principles and some capacity for successful moral reflection." Little concluded that Calvin "has a theory of natural law, let there be no mistake about that. But he is not interested in developing a self-contained, independent doctrine. He has what may be called a 'derivative' theory of natural law, one that always has to be seen in relation to a more inclusive theological and moral design."[23] Without debating the issue, William Bouwsma described several references to Calvin's appeal to natural law in the cosmos and society.[24]

And, finally, in 1990 William Klempa contributed a chapter on Calvin's view of natural law to the volume Timothy George edited called *John Calvin and the Church.* Klempa agreed with those who argued that the frequent references to nature and natural law are not peripheral or casual. But, he insisted, "Calvin never allowed natural knowledge of the moral law any independent adequacy as a guide to moral conduct. Natural law remained an inferior adjunct to the written law."[25]

This brief survey shows that Calvin's theology betrays a certain ambivalence about natural law that has allowed scholars to draw sharply different conclusions. It is somewhat ironic that so much debate has centered on this matter of natural law, since it is one of the few topics in Calvin's thought that were not controversial in his own day. In an intensely polemical age, where every doctrine and practice came under scrutiny, natural law was not a disputed subject. John T. McNeill was absolutely correct in saying that "there is no real discontinuity between the teaching of the Reformers and that of their predecessors with respect to natural law." McNeill points out that "not one of the leaders of the Reformation assails the principle. Instead . . . they all on occasion express a quite ungrudging respect for the natural law implanted in the human heart and seek to inculcate this attitude in their readers."[26]

The modern disputes regarding Calvin's understanding and use of natural law are not, therefore, historical analyses of a sixteenth-century polemic. Both Catholics and Protestants appealed to natural law in the sixteenth century. These modern debates arise not from the study of the Reformation but from interest in the internal coherency of Calvin's thought. Does the concept of natural law fit consistently within the Reformer's theology? Does it contradict other, more explicit themes in his thought? Moreover, ever since the Barth-Brunner controversy, Calvin's view of natural law has been placed within the overriding and vexing problem of theological epistemology: can the fallen mind know or perceive the law of nature? In the following pages, I hope to add some further perspective on this topic by (1) presenting Calvin's most explicit statements about the law of nature, (2) examining this epistemological issue, and (3) suggesting that epistemology is not the only framework within which to comprehend Calvin's references to natural law, for equally important is its role within his doctrine of providence.

WHAT CALVIN SAID

As did his predecessors, Calvin assumed the existence of natural law from Romans 2:14-15: "When the Gentiles who have not the law do by nature what the law requires, they are a law unto themselves, even though they do not have the law. They show that what the law requires is written on their hearts while their conscience also bears witness and their conflicting thoughts accuse or perhaps excuse them. . . ." In a passage stemming originally from the 1536/1539 *Institutes,* Calvin identified the natural law with the Decalogue:

> Now that inward law, which we have described above as written, even engraved on the hearts of all, in a sense asserts the very same things that are to be learned from the Two Tables. . . . Accordingly (because it is necessary both for our dullness and for our arrogance), the Lord has provided us with a written law to give us a clearer witness of what was too obscure in the natural law, shake off our listlessness and strike more vigorously our mind and memory.[27]

Commenting on Romans 2:14-15, Calvin wrote:

> Indeed [Paul] shows that ignorance is uselessly presented as an excuse by the Gentiles since they prove by their own deeds that they have some rule of righteousness: for no nation has so abandoned everything human as to discard all laws. . . all have some conceptions of justice and rectitude which are naturally inborn in the hearts of men. Therefore, they have a law, although they are without law for although they do not have a written law, they are by no means completely destitute of the knowledge of what is right and just. They could not otherwise distinguish between vice and virtue. . . . He contrasts nature to a written law to show that the Gentiles had the natural light of justice, which supplied the place of that law by which the Jews were instructed, so that they were a law unto themselves.[28]

Calvin went on to say regarding verse 15:

> They [the Gentiles] prove that there is imprinted on their hearts a discrimination and judgment by means of which they distinguish between that which is honest and dishonest. . . . they were so mastered by the power of truth that they could not disapprove of it. For why did they institute religious rites, except that they were convinced that God ought to be worshipped. . . . Why were they ashamed of adultery and theft, except that they deemed them evils?[29]

In the *Institutes* (IV.20.16) Calvin explained:

Equity, because it is natural, cannot but be the same for all, and therefore, this same purpose ought to apply to all laws, whatever their object. . . . It is a fact that the law of God which we call the moral law is nothing else than a testimony of natural law and of that conscience which God has engraved on the minds of men. Consequently, the entire scheme of this equity of which we are now speaking has been prescribed in it. Hence this equity alone must be the goal and rule and limit of all laws.[30]

Preaching on Deuteronomy 19:14-15, Calvin said:

This law has been received by men although they had never heard it preached by Moses. Our Lord imprinted upon the hearts of men that which he gave to his people by writing. It is true that it was a special grace when the Lord deigned to take up the office of legislator to the people of Israel. Nonetheless, he did not will that men would be so brutal that they would not have these principles of equity, as they are contained in the Law. . . . It is true that men are indeed blind because of the sin of Adam. But our Lord always left some discretion engraved on their hearts, lest they be able to render themselves inexcusable. . . . Here, then, we ought to teach this conformity which we find between the Law of Moses and all the policies that have reigned in the world among the pagans.[31]

These and similar passages show clearly that Calvin assumed the existence of natural law. The law of nature, containing the natural principles of equity, justice, or rectitude, was imprinted by God on the hearts of all human beings. The Decalogue is a specially accommodated restatement of the law of nature, a restatement that brings a "clearer witness" of that which had become obscure.

KNOWLEDGE OF THE NATURAL LAW

Nonetheless, the existence of natural law in Calvin's thought may raise more problems than it solves. As the various debates have shown, its place in his thinking is far from obvious. The main issue is whether a doctrine of natural law fits coherently into Calvin's theological anthropology, and the debate centers on Calvin's view of the effect of sin on the human mind. The omitted sentences designated by the

ellipsis in the first quotation on Romans 2:14-15 (*Inst.* II.8.1) cited
above reads:

> But man is so shrouded in the darkness of errors that he hardly
> begins to grasp through this natural law what worship is acceptable
> to God. Surely he is very far removed from a true estimate of it.
> Besides this, he is so puffed up with haughtiness and ambition and
> so blinded by self-love that he is yet unable to look upon himself
> and, as it were, to descend within himself, that he may humble and
> abase himself and confess his own miserable condition.[32]

When Calvin spoke of the natural law in this more "formal" manner, he quickly reminded his readers of how natural law served to
render us inexcusable. Sin so corrupted the human mind that we can
no longer have a natural knowledge of God's will or nature. When
Adam fell through a lack of faith in the Word, God ordained that "the
first man should at one and the same time have and lose, both for
himself and his descendants, the gifts that God had bestowed on
him."[33] Those gifts were both supernatural and natural. The supernatural gifts were completely destroyed: namely, faith, the love of God,
charity towards the neighbor, zeal for holiness, and righteousness.[34]
These gifts are "beyond nature" and are restored only through the
work of Christ, which renews the image of God in the soul.

But the *natural* gifts, soundness of mind and uprightness of heart,
were only weakened and corrupted, "not completely wiped out."
Repeatedly Calvin insisted that man did not become a beast in the
Fall. As Barth noted, "even as a sinner, man is a man and not a
tortoise."[35] Calvin could not have said it better: even after the Fall,
human beings retained a mind and a will. The will was no longer free
because it was enslaved to sin, but nonetheless it was still active.
Although the mind was no longer "sound," it was still rational.

But Calvin used several problematic concepts to discuss the abilities
and inabilities of this fallen human being. Not only did we retain a
mind and will, but we also appear to have preserved a conscience and
a "remnant" of the image of God. These terms are puzzling, partly
because Calvin's statements are scattered and imprecise, but more
importantly because they pertain to both the supernatural and the
natural realm; they connect, in some vague way, the fallen mind with
the realm of grace. Yet difficult though they may be, the terms are

important precisely because they bear so heavily on our ability to know the natural law. This is particularly true of the conscience, which Calvin defined in the following way:

> We must take our definition [of the conscience] from the etymology of the word. When men grasp the conception of things with the mind and the understanding they are said "to know," from which the word "knowledge" is derived. Likewise, when men have an awareness of divine judgment adjoined to them as a witness which does not let them hide their sins but arraigns them as guilty before the judgment seat—this awareness is called "conscience." *It is a certain mean between God and man, for it does not allow man to suppress within himself what he knows, but pursues him to the point of making him acknowledge his guilt.*[36]

When connecting the conscience with knowledge of the law of nature, Calvin stressed that the still-functioning conscience can only render us inexcusable:

> The purpose of natural law, therefore, is to render man inexcusable. This would not be a bad definition: natural law is that apprehension of the conscience which distinguishes sufficiently between just and unjust, and which deprives men of the excuse of ignorance while it proves them guilty by their own testimony.[37]

The remaining ability of the conscience to judge between good and evil is part of the "remnant" of the *imago Dei.* According to Calvin, the image of God has its seat in the soul and consists in all things in which human beings excel other animals. On the one hand, Calvin will say that "even though we grant that God's image was not totally annihilated and destroyed . . . yet it was so corrupted that whatever remains is frightful deformity."[38] Yet Calvin admits that "in man's perverted and degenerate nature some sparks still shine."[39] Commenting on John 1:9, he attributed the "light that enlightens every man" not to the reborn alone but to all people:

> But since the evangelist mentions in general, "Every man coming into the world," I prefer the other meaning: that rays from this light are shed upon the whole race of men, as I said. For we know that men have this unique quality above the animals, that they are

endowed with reason and intelligence, and that they bear the distinction between right and wrong engraved on their conscience. Therefore no man exists for whom some awareness of that eternal life does not shine. . . . Let us remember that this is only referring to the common light of nature, a far lowlier thing than faith.[40]

What has fueled much of the debate about Calvin and natural law is the question of how the conscience and the remnant of the image of God now function. How fallen are the natural gifts? Are they a "point of contact"[41] between the human being and God? No. Does the remnant of the divine image only render the human being inexcusable before God? Certainly, with respect to the spiritual realm, human reason, will, conscience, and judgment only render human beings guilty *coram Deo;* these remaining faculties can only deprive us of the excuse of ignorance. On this point Calvin was perfectly clear and consistent; his condemnation of our natural gifts as directed to God was unrelenting.

And yet we repeatedly find in Calvin's writings such phrases as *natura docet, natura dictat,* and *sensus naturae.* He referred to the teaching or dictates of nature, to the natural light, as well as to our natural sense, natural instinct, the conscience, and the judgments taught by nature. His treatises and commentaries are filled with references to the *naturae ordo,* the *lex naturae,* or just *ordo* in general. Furthermore, these references do not all serve the function of condemnation; frequently they also explain the positive aspects still evident in the fallen human world.

These positive references to "nature" and "natural law" are explained by the separation Calvin drew between the natural and spiritual realms. In Calvin's view, the law of nature concurred primarily with the second table of the law. The first table "instructs us in piety and the proper duties of religion by which we are to worship his majesty. The second table prescribes how in accordance with the fear of his name, we ought to conduct ourselves in human society."[42] Calvin believed that human beings "have somewhat more understanding of the precepts of the second table because they are more closely concerned with the preservation of civil society among men."[43]

This moves the discussion to a different set of issues and presuppositions revolving around human conduct within society. Calvin shifted the discussion of the natural law away from one's standing before God to relationships in the world. Nonetheless, this shift did not mean that Calvin had a "secular" morality or a naturalistic context for society. To understand how the apprehension of natural law or the teachings of nature functioned in this aspect of Calvin's thought we must move from the sphere of theological anthropology and epistemology to the sphere of providence.[44]

PROVIDENCE, NATURAL LAW, AND SOCIETAL LIFE

The creation and the Fall were central to Calvin's thinking about the order of nature. He imagined a pre-fallen world characterized by the beauty of order, where all creatures had assigned places and functions. The creation story described in Genesis 1:1-31 proved both the creation *ex nihilo* and the bringing of order out of disorder. In agreement with the exegetical tradition of the Church, Calvin argued that without the constant activity of divine providence, nature would cease to exist or, what is more particularly Calvin's view, would disintegrate into complete disorder. He interpreted Psalm 104:29—"When thou hidest thy face, they [living things] are dismayed; when thou takest away their breath, they die . . ."—to show that any withdrawal of God would reduce nature to nothing. From the time of its formation, the cosmos required the power of God to uphold it. Such sustenance was required not only of that original chaos created by God but also of the order that the Lord established in the six days of creation. In Calvin's view, the order that God gradually brought into being out of chaos was not a stabilizing permanent force that made nature more independent. On the contrary, that order itself was dependent, requiring the direct and powerful providence of God:

> But if that chaos required the hidden inspiration of God lest it suddenly dissolve; how could this order, so fair and distinct, subsist by itself unless it derived strength from elsewhere? Therefore, let the Scriptures be fulfilled, "Send forth Thy Spirit and they shall be created and Thou shalt renew the face of the earth" [Ps. 104:30], and, on the other hand, as soon as the Lord takes away his Spirit all things return to their dust and vanish away.[45]

Keeping Order in the Heavens

This concept of order was central to Calvin's cosmology and to his use and explanation of natural law. Like Melanchthon, he frequently called attention to the order in creation as proof of God, creation, and providence.[46] The order of nature revealed in the cosmos and in society revealed to Calvin the wonder and miracle of the stability, regularity, and continuity of creation.

Calvin always emphasized, however, the inherent *instability* of this order. One of his recurring themes was that only a great and divine power could be responsible for the continuing order found in the world. In passages reminiscent of Cicero, Seneca, and Chrysostom, Calvin called attention to the orderly course of the stars and the heavens in order to demonstrate the continuing presence of divine power.[47]

Most importantly, Calvin used the traditional geocentric cosmology of his age to demonstrate the necessity of providence in a dangerous universe. For example, the fact that the stars did not collide in their vast and winding courses absolutely fascinated Calvin and produced in him a spirit of awe and wonder. His frequent descriptions of the orderly heavens revealed his conviction that, by nature, the stars and planets would collide and create disorder or confusion, and that only God's presence could account for their regularity and harmony. The following passage is one example of Calvin's emphasis on the direct governing presence of God as it is discerned in this preservation of order throughout the revolving heavens:

> The first part of this rule is exemplified when we reflect upon the greatness of the maker who stationed, ordered, and put together this multitude of stars (and nothing more beautiful in appearance can be imagined), who so set and fixed some in their stations so they cannot move; who granted to others a freer course, but so they could not by straying, wander into a further space; who so adjusted the motion of all things so that the days and nights, months, years, and seasons of the year could be measured off; who also so proportioned the inequality of days which we daily observe, so that no confusion occurs. It is so, too, when we observe his power in sustaining so great a mass, in governing the swiftly revolving heavenly system and the like. For these few examples make it

sufficiently clear what it is to recognize God's power in the creation of the world.[48]

Keeping the Waters Within Bounds

In Calvin's thought, nature was more than merely contingent and dependent; it was also precarious. By paying close attention to his use of water imagery, which recurred in his discussions of society, we can see clearly the precarious aspect of creation. Calvin drew on traditional cosmological beliefs to describe God's miraculous preservation of dry land. In agreement with the traditional exegesis of Genesis 1:9, Calvin argued that water is a circular element, lighter than the earth and heavier than the air. He then asked why the waters did not overflow the land, for by nature they should cover the earth. The existence of dry land for human life was evidence of a miracle by God. In order to make room for animals and human society, God's power kept the waters from overflowing the earth. Calvin stressed the divine restraint imposed by God to keep the waters in their bounds. The following quotation from his commentary on Jeremiah 5:22 (in which the Lord says, "I placed the sand as the bound for the sea . . .") recalls the turbulent sea of Genesis 1:2, the belief that creation came about in the midst of a chaotic sea and was therefore surrounded by water (Gen. 1:6-7; Prov. 8:27-29), and the belief that the sea must obey the Lord (Ps. 65:7, 89:9, 114:3). Combining the biblical imagery with his cosmology, Calvin explained that, by nature, water should overwhelm the earth, making the planet uninhabitable by the human race.

. . . for there is nothing more terrible than a tempestuous sea. It appears as if it would overwhelm the whole world when its waves swell with so much violence. . . . But the sea itself, which strikes terror into all, even the most constant, quietly obeys God, for however furious may be its tossings, they are yet restrained. Now if anyone inquires how this can be, it must be a miracle, for no reason can explain this. For we know that the sea, as other elements, is spherical. As the earth is round, so also is the element of water, as well as air and fire. Since, then, the form of this elements is spherical, we must know that it is not lower than the earth, but being lighter shows that it stands above the earth. How is it then that the sea does not immediately overflow the whole earth for it is liquid and cannot stand in one place except restrained by some secret power and impulse of God? Now the word of God, though not heard by us, nor resounding in the air, is yet heard by the sea, for it is confined within its own limits.[49]

Not only did the waters once cover the earth but also, as Genesis 1:6 shows, God suspended some waters in the heavens. Calvin used this traditional theory of lower and supracelestial waters to emphasize the dangerous and threatened position of human beings in the world. The human race, he argued, was surrounded by the waters below and the celestial waters above: "God has purposely placed us between two graves unless in fancied security we should despise that kindness on which our life depends. For the element of water which the philosophers consider one of the principles of life, threatens us with death from above and below except insofar as it is restrained by the hand of God."[50] Interpreting Genesis 1:9 ("Let the waters be gathered together"), Calvin relied on the traditional argument that by his power God continually made room for human beings to live:

This is an illustrious miracle, that the waters by their departure have given a dwelling place to men. For even philosophers concede that the natural position of the waters was to cover the whole earth, as Moses explains that they did at the beginning: first, because being an element it must be circular and because this element is heavier than the air and lighter than the earth, it ought to cover the latter in its whole circumference. But that the seas, being gathered together as in heaps, should yield to man, is seemingly against nature. . . . Let us know, therefore, that we are dwelling on dry ground because by his command God has removed the waters so that they should not submerge the earth.[51]

Keeping Earth Afloat

For Calvin, further proof that God sustained the order of nature was to be seen in the position of the earth. Calvin was acutely aware that the earth is a mass that is heavier than the surrounding elements upon which it appears to rest. Just as Calvin wondered why the stars did not collide and why the waters stayed in their bounds, so too he asked why the earth did not fall down, for nothing inherent in the mass of the earth would secure its floating position. The earth rested only on air and water. Why, then, did not the waters rise above the earth? The only answer he could sustain was that "the providence of God has counteracted the order of nature so that a dwelling place may be found for man . . . nothing in the world is stable except insofar as it is sustained by the hand of God."[52] The waters "are held back in order that man would have some place to live. By nature that cannot be. It is necessary, therefore, that there be some divine providence at work here."[53]

One last quotation will show how Calvin used traditional cosmological theory as proof of divine providence, a providence that sustained both nature and society:

> If we regard the earth, I beg you, upon what is it founded? It is founded upon water and air. . . . We cannot possibly build a house fifteen feet high on firm ground without having to lay a foundation. But look at the whole earth founded upon trembling, indeed poised above such bottomless depths that it might be turned upside down at any moment and become disordered. Hence, there must be a wonderful power of God to keep it in its condition.[54]

The continual wonder that Calvin expressed about the beauties of nature was rooted in his belief that God's presence was seen there upholding, restraining, and ordering creation. In Calvin's view, the inherent character of creation was not conducive to order; only a great divine power could preserve the grand orderliness we perceive in the universe. The order of nature depended on "the continual rejoicing of God in his works." If God ceased to rejoice therein, if he ceased to give vigor to the earth or if he looked upon creation with wrath, the sphere of nature would collapse into disorder. Without God's continual preservation, the stars would collide, the earth would fall down, and waters would gush forth and engulf the earth.

The Forces of Disorder

For Calvin, the cosmos took on a threatening aspect with the Fall because at that time the forces of disorder invaded the world. Calvin's identification of the Fall with disorder is clear from his commentary on Genesis, where he defined Adam's rebellion as "the subversion of all equity and well-constituted order."[55] In the pre-fallen world, all creatures have assigned places: Adam commanded Eve and humans governed the animals. The serpent "overstepped his bounds" when he tempted Eve, and the fall of Adam revealed the "violation of all order," because now human beings have been led into rebellion by one "lower than themselves."[56]

The act of unbelief was, then, an act of disorder among creatures, an act that unleashed disorder into God's previously ordered world. The oneness of the human being with the order of nature is seen in the fact that the Fall affected all of creation. Nature itself was changed because of human sin. After the Fall, the earth was no longer as fertile, and briars and locusts came into being. In Calvin's interpretation, nature did not merely become weakened but actively rebelled against the human race. The elements are now in disorder and threaten human existence. The animals, which were naturally endowed with a submissive spirit, are now wild, savage, and dangerous. The world was created for the comfort and service of human beings, but now the creation has risen up and rebelled against humanity. Scorching heat, the deluge of rains, earthquakes, noxious and savage animals, and terrible winds are all evidence that our sin overturned the order of nature:

> In a word, nothing is certain, but all things are in a state of disorder. . . . We throw heaven and earth into disorder by our sins. For if we were in right order as to our obedience to God, doubtless all the elements would be conformable to us and we should therefore observe in the world, as it were, an angelic harmony.[57]

With the Fall, this beautiful creation took on a threatening countenance; consequently, the forces of disorder are lapping at our heels just as Calvin's waters threatened to engulf the earth. After the Fall, the forces of disorder became so threatening that creation required even more of the restraining providence of God lest it collapse into complete chaos. In his commentary on Romans, Calvin wrote that the whole structure of the world would "dissolve at almost every moment and all of its parts would fail in the sorrowful confusion that followed the fall of Adam, if they were not borne up from elsewhere by some hidden stability."[58]

Not only did disorder penetrate the physical elements of the cosmos, but the historical sphere was also now characterized by an ever-threatening moral disorder. The threatening image of water recurs when Calvin describes this dangerous confusion in human history and society. Human society is now "engulfed by a flood of iniquity which also must be continually restrained lest it rush forth and engulf the earth."[59] Just as the devil subverted legitimate order in the Fall, now the wicked are always trying to create and spread moral disorder in society. According to Calvin, the fall of governments, the moral disobedience against the Decalogue and natural law, and the subsequent chaos in society were to be traced back to the wrath of God evident in all forms of societal confusion.[60] For Calvin, the continual wars, injustices, revolutions, and immoralities present in society were proofs of the moral disorder unleashed after the Fall, a moral disorder that has permeated all of history.

The Bridle of Providence

Calvin's understanding of the sinister and threatening aspect of creation is evident in his use of the image of a "bridle" that reins in those physical and historical forces that endanger nature and society. Just as God restrained and bridled the waters in order to keep them within their appointed bounds, he now must bridle the animals lest they devour people. Most importantly, the Lord must now bridle people lest they devour one another.[61] In Calvin's theology, the "bridle of divine providence" curbs the wicked and the devil lest they succeed in completely overturning all order and making created life unlivable. The fact that Satan had to present himself to God in Job 1:6 proved to Calvin that the Lord was always in sovereign control, bridling the wicked: "with the bridle of his power God holds [Satan] bound and restrained."[62] Calvin's reluctance to rely on the concept of a "permissive will" in God demonstrates his emphasis on the need for the active, continual, and immediate power of divine providence. Calvin's God was no "watchtower" divinity; God never "indolently" permitted nature, history, or society to take a ruinous course. Calvin's God exercised his supreme will and determined all events.[63]

However, creation and history were more than threatening and dangerous: they were also the arena of God's revelation and providence, the "theater of his glory." God not only restrained the forces of disorder inimical to the natural order but also guided history through natural law, governments, and the knowledge acquired by human beings. Hence God preserved and directed the beauty, stability, life, and order of the world.

Calvin's references to the natural law, or the "dictates of nature," are an extension of his doctrine of providence. His primary purpose was not to formulate a "doctrine" of natural law but to appropriate the concept of the *lex naturae* as one way to explain the continuation of order in society after the devastating effects of sin. Natural law was also a providential bridle. Calvin was very conscious of the connection between the preservation of the cosmic realm and the preservation of the social realm. His statements about the law of nature and society reveal his twofold attitude toward creation and history: fear of an ever-threatening disorder and chaos, and awe before the continuation of stability and order.

Calvin explained this continuation of society after the Fall precisely in terms of an order imposed by the restraint of "nature." Continually he depicted a world held in check by God where men and women were able to conduct their temporal lives without falling into a "bestial confusion." Therefore, Calvin did not emphasize only the external restraint by God; he also assumed that ordered, civilized life in society could flourish because of the remaining natural instincts, perceptions, and abilities present in man's soul. The ability of human beings to recognize the truths of natural law was a means whereby people could still participate in the formation of government and a stable civic life. According to Calvin, it is the human conscience that recognizes the need for order taught by natural law.[64] Calvin connected natural law to the "witness," "monitor," or "testimony" of the conscience: "The law of God which we call the moral law is nothing else than that natural law and that conscience which God has engraved upon the minds of men."[65] A remnant of the *imago Dei*, the human conscience condemns us before God when we disobey the teachings of natural law and thereby threaten to throw society into more confusion. But the conscience and the knowledge of the law of nature can also conserve society by distinguishing good from evil, equity from injustice, and order from disorder.[66]

Calvin's statements regarding the natural discernment of the conscience have three general themes: the natural impulse for unity or the formation of society, the instinct for order in society and the family, and the necessity for an ordered civil government. Included in the latter are Calvin's comments about law, property, and the wisdom of the pagans. Throughout these discussions, the human being's discernment of natural law functions as an internal bridle that fosters and preserves society.

The Natural Impulse Toward Society

In Calvin's interpretation, God created Adam and Eve in order that there might be "human beings on earth who cultivate mutual society among themselves." Recorded in the book of Genesis, this beginning of human society exemplified the general principle that man was formed to be a social animal. The natural impulse toward the formation of society inclined people to care for the human race as a whole. · Nature, Calvin argued, causes us to feel for one another, since "we are inclined to mercy by some hidden impulse of nature." For Calvin, murder was not only criminal but abhorrent to our natural instincts; since we are all made in the image of God, murder is contrary to the order of nature and to our "natural sentiment."[67]

· Calvin also believed that the preservation of the human race was engraved in human nature and a part of natural law. He interpreted Judah's instructions to Onan to go to his brother's wife as an "instinct of nature" whereby people were disposed naturally toward preserving the race.[68] Even the pagans recognized the natural inclination toward unity and preservation, since they knew by nature that all people were born for the sake of one another.[69] Calvin believed that the pagans also taught that the bonds of human society had to be maintained by mutual sharing. Throughout such discussions, Calvin relied on the integrity of human natural perceptions and instincts to account for the continued ordered existence of society, for "since man is by nature a social animal, he tends through natural instinct to foster and preserve society. Consequently we observe that there exist in all men's minds, universal impressions of a certain civic fair dealing and order."[70]

Order in the Family

These "universal impressions" manifested themselves for Calvin in the bonds of marriage and family and in the submission to civil authorities and the rule of law. The original bonds of marriage and family ties were engraved in the eternal and inviolable law of nature and were therefore understandable by all people without any special divine revelation. For Calvin, the "order of nature" taught that the woman should be the man's helper and willingly "be subservient to him."[71] Calvin also taught that adultery and promiscuity, which would destroy the family, not only violated the morality commanded by Scripture but were contrary to the "dictates of nature." "We gather, besides, from the words of Abimelech, that all nations have impressed on their minds the sentiment that the violation of holy wedlock is a crime worthy of divine vengeance and, therefore, they have a fear of the judgment of God."[72] Monogamy is inviolable and recognized by all societies, "for the ignorant souls who had only natural understanding and behaved as their judgment directed them, have they not known that the wife was, as it were, a part of the husband and that there exists an inseparable bond between them so that they ought not to forsake each other unless they want to tear themselves to pieces?"[73]

Polygamy, adultery, and incest are immoral, "against nature," and contrary to the divinely established order known through natural law. These unnatural acts also, Calvin argued, threaten to reduce people to the level of beasts. Polygamy is "disordered" and "confused." Adulterers are like neighing horses, "for where such lasciviousness prevails, men degenerate into beasts."[74] For Calvin, the "pure sentiment of nature" condemned adultery, which threatened the safety and stability of society.[75] And, by nature, "all men were instilled with a great horror of incest and natural reason judged it abhorrent for Judah to lie with Tamar."[76] Incestuous marriages, Calvin stated, "trample upon all the laws of nature," and the horror of incest stemmed from the "natural feelings implanted in us by God." Even the "barbarism" of the East, Calvin insisted, could not nullify the law against incest, for "what is natural cannot be abrogated by any consent and custom. In short, the prohibition of incest here set forth is by no means among those laws which are commonly abrogated according to the circumstances of time and place, since it flows from the fountain of nature itself and is founded on the general principle of all laws, which is perpetual and inviolable."[77] A king could not command an incestuous marriage, "for no legislator can effect that a thing which nature pronounces to be vicious should not be vicious; and if tyrannical arrogance dares to attempt it, the light of nature will presently shine forth and prevail. . . . even among the heathen nations this law, as if engraved and implanted on the hearts of men, was seen as indissoluble."[78]

Civil Order and Government

For Calvin, then, family ties among husband, wife, and children were grounded in the law of nature and recognized through natural reason.[79] These same appeals to "nature" recurred in Calvin's arguments about civil government. Throughout his political discussions Calvin called on "nature," the "wisdom of the pagans," and the natural principles of justice and equity. "What then," Calvin asked,

> shall we deny that the truth shone upon the ancient jurists who established civic order and discipline with such great equity. . . . those men whom Scripture calls "natural men" were, indeed, sharp and penetrating in their investigation of the things below. Accordingly, let us learn by their example how many gifts the Lord left to human nature even after it was despoiled of its true good.[80]

Calvin often called on Plato, Seneca, and Cicero as authorities for his views of civic order and government. To defend his view of a combined democracy and aristocracy he employed Plato's analysis of the types and dangers of different forms of governments.[81] He also cited Plato as teaching that no one was qualified to govern a commonwealth unless appointed by God.[82] Seneca knew that the magistrate was the "father of his country" and must be obeyed.[83]

Most importantly, Calvin thought that the pagans recognized by nature the importance of laws. The art of government and the science of jurisprudence were handed down from the pagans, and Cicero taught that laws were the sinews of the state. Calvin prefaced his remarks about laws in the *Institutes* by saying:

> Next to the magistracy in the civil state come the laws, stoutest sinews of the commonwealth, or as Cicero, after Plato, calls them, the souls without which the magistracy cannot stand, even as they themselves have no force apart from the magistracy. Accordingly, nothing truer could be said than that the law is a silent magistrate, the magistrate a living law.[84]

Repeatedly Calvin relied on the "wisdom of the ancients" to support the naturally known necessity for a strong and stable government, obedience to rulers, and the rule of law.

For Calvin, the rule of law, or "order of justice," corresponded to the natural sense in the human being that recognizes the need for order. Nature itself taught that human lives must be governed by law and ruled by the principles of equity and justice. The human conscience still retained insight into the natural principles of equity and justice and was thereby able to order society so that it could survive.

In Calvin's discussions about the particular tasks or rules of government, arguments from natural equity were combined with arguments based on the threat of confusion. It was Calvin's belief that the rights of property and the necessity for boundaries were to be guarded carefully or else everything would dissolve into confusion or disorder. Against the communism held by some Anabaptists and Libertines, Calvin insisted that God manifested his goodness in assigning territory to each nation and private property to each individual.[85] These "fanatics," Calvin exclaimed, who wanted to hold all things in common would overthrow the entire civil order and throw everything into confusion. Even the pagans knew by nature that the right of property must be observed, for otherwise "there would be no equity among men and everything would be confused."[86]

> But insofar as we have seen this principle which nature always taught, namely, that if boundaries were not held and observed, there would have been a horrible confusion among men and no laws would have been observed. . . . for when someone wished to enlarge his own, it is as if he violated the order of nature. See, then, God who has distinguished peoples in order that all might live, communicating one with another in order that there may be no disordered confusion. See, therefore, how each person ought to be content with his limits.[87]

Argumentation of this sort recurs frequently throughout Calvin's writings. If the order of nature was violated, society would fall into confusion. The natural order and "sense of justice" taught that murder, false testimony, broken contracts, and dishonesty in business were against the order of nature and threatened to return the whole race to "the common confusion of all."[88] The natural mind's percep-

tion of the unchanging law of nature corresponded to the constant
need for order and restraint to enable society to continue after the
Fall. Such natural insights kept the human race from falling to the
level of beasts. Consequently, society or civilization was preserved
both by God's restraint of nature, wickedness, and rebellion, and by
human natural insights into the law of nature, all of which prevented
the fall into anarchy.

Concluding Observations

The debates about natural law have largely revolved around the issue
of the noetic effect of sin in Calvin's thought. In terms of theological
epistemology, the issue of natural law is somewhat problematic. As
my essay has shown, I am mainly in sympathy with Beyerhaus, Brunner, Gloede, and others who argued for the existence of natural law
in Calvin's theology and believed that the remnant of the image of
God ensured that even fallen human beings retained some knowledge
of the law of nature. The question, as I see it, has to do with the
function of this knowledge. In matters of salvation, our innate awareness of natural law only renders us inexcusable. Nonetheless, this
inexcusability rests not only on our inability to claim innocence but
on the bondage of our wills. Knowledge of either the natural or the
written law did not, according to Calvin, give us the ability to obey.
Within the realm of salvation, this ability is effected only by the grace
of Christ. Thus Calvin vehemently criticized those who would deduce
free will from the existence and knowledge of either a natural or a
written law.

However, with reference to the lower earthly realm, Calvin re-
counted the positive effect of our innate understanding of the law of
nature. These positive statements belong, most properly, not to the
discussion of salvation or the knowledge of God, but to the discussion
of providence and the continuation of civilization after the Fall.

Within the context of providence, we can see that throughout his
writings Calvin adopted the common teachings about natural law. He
assumed the existence of the law of nature, whose author was God.
He believed that after the Fall, God made this law clearer through the
written form of the Decalogue. He argued that all people had certain

conceptions of justice and rectitude inborn in their minds by which they naturally recognized the need for justice, law, and order. Calvin did not formulate a "doctrine" of natural law and did not develop a "theology of natural law." Nonetheless, he used the principle of natural law as an extension of his doctrine of providence to explain the survival of civilization.

This context places natural law in the dialectic of order and disorder. On the one hand, Calvin believed that the disorder caused by sin required God to restrain those natural and human forces that threatened to annihilate the human race. God exercised this restraint because he continued to love his own image in the human being and to take joy in his works of creation. Remaining true to his own purposes in creation, God preserved the stability and order of the created realm. The restraint required for societal life was also exercised inwardly through the recognition of natural law by the conscience. According to Calvin, the "dictates" or "insights" of nature prevented men and women from falling into a bestial confusion. He frequently appealed to "nature" in a recurring method of argumentation: the natural mind still perceived the need for order and restraint. For Calvin, natural perception of the law of nature prevented people from killing one another, disobeying laws, committing adultery and incest, breaking contracts, stealing, lying under oath, rebelling against familial and governmental superiors, and abolishing private property. Such natural instincts served as an internal bridle, so to speak, to keep in check those sinful, chaotic forces of lust and greed that lurk within fallen human nature.

The survival of a remnant of the divine image in the fallen soul helped Calvin account for the continuation of society in two ways. He believed that God preserved society because he continued to love his image in the human being. Also, however, the conscience and the "natural light" of reason contributed to the order and stability of the civil realm. Not only did these remnants of the divine image act as a bridle, but they also had a positive function in the instincts of nature that went beyond the idea of restraint. Nature caused human beings to propagate the race, care for children, and even to recognize the image of God or a common human nature in our neighbor. Calvin always insisted on a Christian realism about societal life. This realism required both a respect for the real threat of chaos and an appreciation for the continuing order in the cosmos and in society.

Two further points are important for a full understanding of Calvin's use of natural law. First, while I have emphasized the role of restraint in Calvin's understanding of natural law as it functions within his doctrine of providence, he also gives it a somewhat more positive role. The Reformer adopted the traditional identification of natural law with the moral law of the Decalogue. The question of the knowledge of unredeemed reason concerns God's governance between the Fall and Mt. Sinai as well as the knowledge of the Gentiles. But if the natural law in written revealed form is taken into account, then the obedience to God's moral law has a very positive function, namely, the renewal and reordering of the self and society. Calvin argues that the Decalogue was written in negative form but commands the opposite goodness. Therefore, the command "Thou shalt not kill" both prohibits murder and commands the Christian to act toward his neighbor according to the rule of love. Hence if we look at the Church and natural law, now grounded in the clearer, written law, then the divine law is both a restraint and an active reordering in love of the image of God and the created order.

Second, the use of historical theology for contemporary thought is always somewhat problematic. Contemporary thinkers must recognize that Calvin's use of natural law presupposed certain crucial assumptions that are simply no longer available today in the search for public discourse. These include the following:

1. Calvin could assume that there was an objective reality not dependent on or formed by the human mind. Our time is permeated with the assumption that reality (including moral reality) and meaning are constituted by human cultural perception.

2. Calvin could assume the existence of Christendom and the absolute superiority of Christianity over all other forms of religion. He could, therefore, presuppose certain universal realities that were a part of Christian discourse—for example, sin, human nature, moral universals, and providence—and could assume a theological discourse known by all.

3. As constitutive of his belief in providence, Calvin understood there to be a teleological or ultimate purpose within creation and history.

4. Calvin assumed the "exegetical optimism" of the early reformation.[89] Language, the words of Scripture, had a force and clarity in-

dependent of the human mind, both as a means to truth and as a principle of authority.

5. Finally, I believe that Calvin never fully absorbed the effects of the historicity that was coming to birth in the Renaissance and found its fullest sixteenth-century expression in a figure such as Montaigne.[90] This historicity awakened a deep awareness of one's distance from the past and an acute sense of relativism.

A Response

Timothy George

In September 1909, Karl Barth, fresh from his studies at Marburg, moved to Geneva and under took his first ministerial charge as *pasteur suffragant* to the German-speaking congregation there. That year marked the 400th anniversary of the birth of John Calvin, and Geneva was abuzz with celebrations of the Reformation. In that same year Barth acquired a complete set of Calvin's works in the *Corpus Reformatorum* edition. During the next ten years Barth would discover a "strange new world within the Bible," and would launch a theological revolution that shook Protestant Christianity to its roots. Only years later, after he had begun to prepare lectures for his students at Göttingen, did Barth began to delve deeply into the Calvin volumes he had acquired in 1909.

In a letter to his friend Eduard Thurneysen on June 8, 1922, Barth described his fresh encounter with the Genevan Reformer:

> The little bit of "Reformed theology" that I teach is really nothing in comparison to the trumpet blast which needs to be blown in our sick time. . . . Calvin is a cataract, a primeval forest, a demonic power, something directly down from Himalaya, absolutely Chinese, strange, mythological; I lack the means, the suction cups, even to assimilate this phenomenon, not to speak of presenting it adequately. What I receive is only a thin little stream and what I can then give out again is only a yet thinner extract of this little stream. I could gladly and profitably set myself down and spend all the rest of my life just with Calvin.[1]

Timothy George is the dean of Beeson Divinity School, Samford University, in Birmingham, Alabama, and a senior editor of *Christianity Today*. He is the author of *Theology of the Reformers* and the editor of *John Calvin and the Church: A Prism of Reform*.

77

Of course, Barth went on to share the rest of his life with some other people as well, not the least of whom was Luther. But his comment does point to the ability of Calvin both to fascinate and to perplex. Calvin has been, and remains, a source of engagement but also bafflement on a whole front of issues. Among these is natural law. He whose motto as a master teacher of Holy Scripture was *claritas et brevitas* bequeathed a legacy of ambiguity rather than *claritas* on what has been deemed a most significant issue in the history of Christian thought.

Professor Schreiner has accomplished four things in her very impressive paper: she has surveyed the scholarly debate on natural law, isolated certain programmatic statements of Calvin on this theme, examined the epistemological implications of these statements, and shifted the discussion from the noetic realm to the larger context of Calvin's doctrine of providence. I shall comment briefly on each of these four steps, and then pose a couple of questions of my own.

Calvin and Natural Law

1. *The Scholarly Debate.* Building on an earlier survey by William Klempa, Professor Schreiner gives us a sampling of the scholarly discussion on natural law in the twentieth century. As I look at this literature, it falls into four distinct periods.

The first series of studies was published around the time of the Calvin festivities in 1909. The French and German scholars Lang, Beyerhaus, and Doumergue were eager to find in Calvin a kind of justification for the *Kulterprotestantismus* that prevailed in Europe before the guns of August 1914 shattered forever the equilibrium of the old order. I would place Ernst Troeltsch in this same era even though his major work, *The Social Teachings of the Christian Churches,* was published somewhat later.

A second spate of writings appeared in the early 1930s. Josef Bohatec provided the most substantive interaction with Calvin in his *Calvin und das Recht,* a work that can still be studied with profit today. However, it was the famous clash between Karl Barth and Emil Brunner, and their epigones, that garnered most of the headlines. Obviously the context here was the rise of National Socialism and the emergence of the Confessing Church, which reacted to the brand of *theologia naturalis* put forth by the German Christians. The first article of the Barmen Declaration epitomizes this wholesale rejection of natural theology:

> Jesus Christ, as he has testified to us through the Holy Scripture, is the one Word of God, whom we are to hear, whom we are to trust and obey in life and in death. We repudiate the false teaching that the church can and must recognize yet other happenings and powers, images and truths as divine revelation along side this one Word of God, as a source of her preaching.[2]

A third flurry of interest in natural law occurred in the aftermath of World War II, and the studies of McNeill, Torrance, Parker, and Dowey all belong to this period. To some extent we hear here a delayed echo of the Barth/Brunner exchange. But the center of scholarly discussion has shifted from continental Europe to the British and American scene. These scholars were leading academics in countries that were taking the lead in the reconstruction of Europe. In a world beset by the threat of the Cold War, the discussion of natural law was part of an ongoing search for stabilizing principles in an epoch of threatening chaos.

A fourth series of articles appeared during the sixties and seventies. The work of Arthur Cochrane, David Little, and Fred Graham was published against the backdrop of campus upheaval, anti-war demonstrations, Watergate, and other societal turmoil. Significantly, Fred Graham's book was entitled *Calvin: Constructive Revolutionary*.

Now, in the mid-nineties, we have come together under the rubric "Catholics and Evangelicals in Conversation about Natural Law." The publication of the statement "Evangelicals and Catholics Together" in 1994, and the growing recognition among Roman Catholics and evangelicals of a vested co-belligerency on an array of moral concerns, inform the dialogue we carry on today. I myself am committed to this common witness, but it remains to be seen whether Calvin can be mined as a major resource for our collaboration.

2. *Calvin's Statements.* Professor Schreiner next presents representative statements from Calvin that incorporate the language of natural law, citing two from the *Institutes,* one from the Romans commentary, and one from a sermon on Deuteronomy. Such quotations could be multiplied many times over, but in fact the passages she has chosen illustrate this theme very well. Pulling them together, we can construct a composite definition of natural law for Calvin:

Calvin's definition of NL

■ Natural law is God's law, not an autonomous principle or theory.
■ Natural law is universal, "engraved on the hearts of all."
■ The content of natural law is the moral law as revealed in the Decalogue.
■ The intention or "goal and rule" of natural law is equity, traces of which may be seen in the various political structures of humankind, all of which contain "some rule of righteousness."

3. *Epistemological Focus.* Professor Schreiner rightly points out that much of the debate on natural law in Calvin has focused on the epistemological/anthropological issue of the effect of the Fall on the primeval deposit of natural revelation. Indeed, this is where the debate between Barth and Brunner became sticky. In his famous retort to Brunner, Barth pointed out that the entire structure of Book I of the *Institutes* hinges on a significant hypothetical statement, one that undergirds Calvin's discussion of the *duplex cognitio dei:* "I do not yet touch on the knowledge of God the Redeemer revealed in Christ the Mediator, but I speak only of the primal and simple knowledge to which the very order of nature would have let us *if Adam had remained upright.*" In citing this quotation against Brunner, Barth italicized the concluding clause in the original Latin: *si integer stetisset Adam.* Thus natural theology is an objective possibility created by God, but not a subjective reality open to sinful human beings in a fallen world.

True enough, the image of God, though horribly deformed, has not been completely destroyed. The "worm of conscience," sharper than a cauterizing iron, gnaws away within every human heart. The *semen religionis* remains. This seed has been so corrupted, however, that it produces only the worst fruits. The question remains whether this divine deposit can yet yield a sufficient basis for a minimalist morality in human society, despite the fact that the overriding value of the natural knowledge of God in a post-lapsarian world is the cultivation of culpability.

Professor Schreiner believes that an undue emphasis on the epistemological issue has skewed scholarly discussion of natural law in Calvin. The framing of the question, she thinks, reflects preoccupation with a twentieth-century theological problem rather than a burning concern of the sixteenth-century Reformation. She prefers to place the discussion of natural law in the context of Calvin's doctrine of providence.

4. *Providence and Natural Law.* Building on her own excellent book *The Theater of His Glory: John Calvin and the Natural Order,* Professor Schreiner deals first with God's governance of the cosmos, and then with God's guidance in history and human society. One of her themes is the dynamism of God's providential activity in the natural realm. The God of Calvin is no mere *deus otiosus,* no lazy God who observes the world from the lofty distance of a watchtower, no absentee landlord who merely "permits" things to happen. He is rather an interventionist God who doesn't mind getting his hands dirty in the daily operation of the cosmos. Over against this theme of God as an activist agent is the countervailing theme of chaos, danger, and threat within the created realm. In this context, then, natural law functions as a "bridle" to restrain and constrict the destructive impulses in the world.

When we move from the cosmic to the societal realm, from nature to history, we are confronted with Calvin's comments about the natural instinct for an ordered familial, social, and civic life. It is certainly true that Calvin thought human beings could learn a great deal about this-worldly flourishing from natural law. However, a minimal standard of justice for public policy was never his driving concern. In the first edition of the *Institutes* (1536), we hear the note that was to dominate Calvin's political theology: "Not only does government provide for men's living together but it also prevents idolatry, sacrilege against God's name, blasphemies against his truths and other public offenses against religion."[3] Calvin spoke of the magistracy as a *sacrum ministerium* and criticized the Lutherans for regarding magistrates only as a kind of necessary evil.

Natural law was neither a necessary nor a sufficient guide for Christian magistrates in the performance of their God-given duties. At best, natural law might provide a kind of negative incentive for these ministers of divine justice. Thus in commenting on the Seventh Commandment Calvin declares, "By the universal law of the Gentiles, the punishment for adultery was always death; wherefore it is all the more base and shameful in Christians not to imitate at least the heathens. Adultery is punished no less severely by the *lex Julia* than by the law of God."[4]

Concluding Observations

Professor Schreiner observes that natural law was not a focus of controversy between Protestants and Catholics in the sixteenth century. But she minimizes the discontinuity between Calvin and his medieval predecessors on this matter. While it is certainly true that Calvin did not attack the medieval tradition of natural law as he did the Catholic doctrine of transubstantiation or the cult of relics, a nuance in an ideological difference can be a chasm. Both Luther and Calvin significantly qualified the tradition of natural theology received from medieval Scholastic theology. For example, neither showed any interest in demonstrations of the existence of God. In another area of dogmatic development, both rejected the declaration of the Fifth Lateran Council on the philosophical provability of the natural immortality of the soul. We should not be surprised that the biblical positivism of the Reformers mitigated against their assimilation of a robust doctrine of natural law.

Is it possible to extrapolate out of Calvin a doctrine of natural law that can serve as a grammar of public discourse today without doing violence to his own intentions? While Professor Schreiner's discussion of Calvin's doctrine of providence brings needed light to a much neglected vortex of his thought, I am not sure that moving the question from the noetic to the cosmic and historic realms really helps us here. While for Calvin God's sovereign rule is surely present *etiam extra ecclesiam,* the doctrine of providence in the total structure of his thought is much more closely related to election and ecclesiology, what later theologians called "special providence," which in turn issues in the kind of distinctive piety reflected in the first question of the Heidelberg Catechism, "What is thy only comfort in life and in death?"

It has been pointed out that contemporary Christians concerned with influencing public policy could pursue one of three options: evangelization, coercion, and the quest for common ground in the interests of a shared agenda. Calvin was clearly a strong advocate of the first option, evangelization. Under his direction, the Company of Pastors in Geneva trained and exported hundreds of missionaries into his native France, and, some sixty years before the Pilgrims arrived at Plymouth, they also sponsored an ill-fated evangelical mission to

Brazil. But Calvin was not adverse to use of the second option, coercion, in implementing the aims of the Kingdom of God in the earthly realm. Indeed, Calvinism became a potent revolutionary force in international politics precisely because of this religio-political commitment. As for the third option, there is precious little in Calvin's treatment of natural law to serve as common ground for a public policy agenda.

But there may still be a fourth way, the option of an intentional community of faith set over against its environing culture, a company of men and women who bear faithful witness in the name of him whose crown rights can never be assimilated to the kingdoms and societies of this world. Calvin in his letters of counsel to minority refugee churches that labored for the glory of God is a mentor for this model of Christian community. While we should not abandon legitimate dimensions of the first three options, I submit that Christians today can best shape the public policy of their society by refusing to reduce the faith to the religion of the *polis,* whether that religion be based on natural or positive law.

Comments

Susan Schreiner: To say, as I have said, that Calvin appropriated natural law without controversy does not mean that he appropriated it without difference. I think that if we had in front of us a full-blown history of natural law theory and use among the canonists, among medieval theologians, and the like, we would find that in comparison to the tradition Calvin uses the doctrine of natural law almost casually, and with different purposes in mind. He certainly does not use it in terms of the immortality of the soul or proof of the existence of God. We are not dealing with a continuum here. Frankly, Calvin quite often assumed he knew a lot more about the medieval tradition than he really did.

As to whether we can extrapolate a doctrine of natural law from Calvin by moving from the epistemological to the providential: I'm not sure that we can extract a doctrine of natural law from Calvin one way or another. Let me say two things. First, I do not think that the question of epistemology is a purely twentieth-century one. The sixteenth century was obsessed with theological epistemology. It was an age that, if it did nothing else, sought religious epistemological certitude with a vengeance. I think the Reformers made that quest much more difficult by their emphasis on the noetic effect of sin.

Second, all I'm saying about the Brunner-Barth debate, which is a debate I deeply respect, is that it may not be the only way to figure out how Calvin is using the terms *conscience* and *imago Dei*. I think there are other ways of getting at how he actually uses natural law. Not dogmatically but in a truly utilitarian manner, it answers for him a question about why order continues to exist in the world. Calvin's most numerous references to natural law are outside the *Institutes*.

Note: The participants in this conversation are identified on pages 173-74.

84

When you leave the systematic work behind and turn to the sermons and commentaries, Calvin's references to natural law occur most often in his discussion of how the Fall brought on disorder: You're lucky to be alive; why are you alive if you are not redeemed? The reason you're alive is that left in your fallen, miserable mind is an instinct for natural law that preserves human society. Calvin is awestruck by it and is using that to shame you. Functionally, particularly outside the *Institutes,* this works within the overarching theme of providence.

David Coffin: I have to confess that I don't see as clearly where the epistemological problem lies. It seems to me that Calvin uses natural law precisely to resolve the seeming conflict between the doctrine of sin and the preservation of the world. God has established order in the world, but sin has darkened the mind so that you don't have human flourishing, you don't have human beings joyfully serving the Lord through this natural light. A "natural" religious knowledge of God was possible for Adam. But now, within the fallen order, what this natural knowledge provides is not a saving knowledge of God and of how we ought to live and flourish, but this guilt-producing, re-straining function that I think is absolutely critical to Calvin's theology.

Remember, though Calvin insists that natural law has this restrain-ing, somewhat directing function, the problem is that sin keeps leading to darkness. He argues then that the moral law and the revelation of God bring light. But even Scripture's light itself doesn't illumine the sinful heart and mind. That requires a special work of the Spirit of God. Over time Scripture's own light would be put out by the sin-fulness of men and women. For Calvin, Scripture is not intrinsically more effectual in achieving its end than natural law; it's only that the Spirit blesses the Word of God so that it leads to a saving knowledge of Jesus Christ. Then all of the light, both Scripture's light and the light of natural law, can lead to this reconstruction in the redeemed community.

As to the possibility of a third agenda in Calvin: I agree that Calvin wants to see the magistrate in a way that would make me not at all enthusiastic about having him become my pastor; but I don't think it's integral to Calvin's use of natural law that he expects there to be a Christian magistrate. In fact, for him natural law gives an account of how the world is preserved *without* the Christian magistrate. Where there isn't a Christian magistrate, this is what God is doing to preserve the world, to restrain sin and lead to some possibility of human flourishing, but only in a this-worldly sense. The human way is still sinful; it's just less sinful than it would be if people abandoned such things as faithfulness in marriage, doing proper work, and abiding by contracts.

Susan Schreiner: Your point about the magistrate fits into what I was trying to say. Whenever you read Calvin you have to ask, "Which sphere are we talking about? Are we talking about the divine perspective, the human perspective, the redeemed perspective, the sinful perspective, before the law, after the law, before Christ, after Christ?" I do think that what he says about the Christian magistrate is critical to his thinking. But I also think that it means we are there dealing with the perspective that says, We now have the Decalogue, and we have Christianity. When he refers to the pagans and the insights of the pagans—and he was more than aware that judicial principles came down to us from the pagans—then we are not dealing with a Christian magistrate, but we still have to answer, in his mind, the question of why we have these principles, and why we have an ordered society that, though it stumbles along, still survives.

Deal Hudson: Can the third option for Christians who want to influence public policy be called rational persuasion—evangelism, coercion, and rational persuasion?

David Coffin: That third option isn't only rational persuasion, though it certainly includes that. I may well know the truth, and be persuaded of it, and not do it. I need something more than rational persuasion, some internal disposition to follow that truth. It seems to me that Calvin is saying that the vestigial remains of the image of God in man lead him to want to flourish, to order his life out of self-interest, and that God has put principles in the world that reinforce that desire to flourish. The mind perceives such principles, and the person then orders his or her life in order to gain his own ends. The good works that ensue are not saving, they are not in any way acceptable to God of themselves. But God uses them, and this disposition to follow the truth, to preserve the world.

Susan Schreiner: You must always be careful with Calvin about rational persuasion. You must not underestimate the power of sin on the mind. The radical effect of sin on reason is a belief that Luther, Zwingli, and Calvin all shared. Calvin might be very suspicious of our discussions here about what we can rationally persuade or rationally prove. Luther called reason the devil's whore. He could hardly have put it any stronger than that. In Luther it's made even worse by the fact that the devil is so seductive and acts in accordance with fallen reason.

Half of the time when you're reading Calvin you have no idea whether this person he's talking about is living in this wonderfully rational world of delusion, or whether he's talking about a redeemed reason. The idea of a redeemed reason is important, but that is a mess, because everybody in the sixteenth century is claiming the illumination of the Spirit. Frankly, I think the exegetical optimism of the Reformation came to a crashing halt on the words, "This is my body." Reason is a problem in the sixteenth century.

David Coffin: It seems to me that it's critical to the discussion to maintain the distinction between the formal capacity of reason to function in the temporal order, and the material capacity of reason to lead one savingly to God. That distinction between knowledge and saving knowledge significantly illumines Calvin's discussion. It leaves a use of the mind in the fallen order, wickedly . . .

Deal Hudson: Imperfectly.

David Coffin: Wickedly, under the judgment of God. "The plowing of the wicked is an abomination to the Lord." It's good plowing. The wicked use their minds carefully to set those courses well, and things grow, and we profit from it. But it's an abomination to the Lord, because the mind is being used out of the sinful disposition of the heart, in correspondence with the principles of the world. That seems to me to be a coherent account of Calvin's position.

John West: First, a point about Calvin: It seems to me that there is another implicit way in which he promotes the use of a natural moral understanding, and that is by the way he depreciates the use of the

Bible to form public policy. I'm thinking particularly of his discussions of punishment. Some Christian reconstructionists today seek support in Calvin for legislating the Old Testament law here, when in fact that is exactly what he says you shouldn't do. Just because the Bible says you should punish murderers with death, that doesn't mean you should do that in your society, given your particular circumstances.

But if the Bible doesn't give you that guidance, what does? It seems to be something more related to the sense of equity, some sort of reasonable sense of morality that I think can be tied to some of his other discussions about natural law. In fact, it almost points to why he doesn't have the elaborate system of natural law that you find in Catholic writers. Calvin's use of natural moral understanding is really more akin to natural right or the classical understanding of natural justice, in that it provides these general principles of right, but the idea of prudence, of applying it to particular circumstances, is also extremely important.

My second point: Susan Schreiner said that natural law really wasn't a matter of controversy between Protestants and Catholics during Calvin's time. I would say the same thing about the American scene, definitely up to the Civil War and possibly after. If you read Protestant writers from the American founding at least up through the Civil War, you find they had no problem with the idea of a natural moral understanding. There was quite a bit of friction between Protestants and Catholics in nineteenth-century America, but this wasn't one of the issues they debated.

Susan Schreiner: I think Calvin's unwillingness to use Scripture as a blueprint for law was due in part to his growing awareness of the distance between the sixteenth century and the ancient world. That awareness became much more pronounced in someone like Montaigne, and Calvin never fully absorbed it in the sense that Montaigne did. Nonetheless, those discussions about the refusal to use the Bible that way do point to Calvin's own humanist sensibilities. Then he's left with finding something else.

Russell Hittinger: Susan Schreiner made some excellent points about what Calvin could assume: objective reality, universals, Christendom—there was a setting in which theological discourse could take place. What I want to propose is that we have inherited a category of theory and ideology that is shaped by people who made these assumptions. I think the only way to make natural law a common grammar today is to try to raise the culture back up to a position where you can talk to it even in weakly Christian or weakly theistic terms. I'm not sure that any of us, Protestant or Catholic, are willing to do that today in our own kind of political order, or if we're willing, that we know how to do it.

John Courtney Murray talked about this very problem, that there could come a day when even the kind of weakly theistic natural law that the American founding relied upon could no longer be assumed, when the common language about these things would be gone, and the project would collapse. Murray seemed to think that Catholics would pick it up at that point, but the last forty years have shown us that that is a problematic assumption.

Luis Lugo: A question for Timothy George: When you located the different phases of scholarship on Calvin and the natural law historically, you said that today we're having this discussion again. What would cause this question to re-emerge?

Timothy George: I simply had in mind that the people gathered at this table represent convictional religious communities, meeting under the heading, "Evangelicals and Catholics in Conversation. . . ." The 1994 document "Evangelicals and Catholics Together" has received a lot of play. There is a sense of co-belligerency on a lot of issues between convictional Christians of Roman Catholic and evangelical Protestant traditions. Now whether we're just a little cocoon of specialists, or whether we could talk about this on Capitol Hill and get anybody to listen, is a question. I'm a little pessimistic about the possibility of the latter.

Luis Lugo: I also found very interesting your introducing the role of the magistrate. Let me suggest, however, that resolving the question of the magistrate's appropriate role, particularly in the matter of preventing offenses against true religion, cannot be done simply on the basis of Calvin's view of natural law. It also has to do with his institutional understanding of the polity in contrast to the Church. Even before you come to the question of natural law, even if you remain within the realm of biblical law, the question is, where do you ground the polity?

I suggest that Calvin's problem here is his failure to sufficiently differentiate the civic community and the believing community. I'm not willing to concede to the theonomist that either you adopt a natural law perspective or you must look to the Old Testament theocracy as the model. I think a good case can be made biblically that we ought to be thinking of the civic community as grounded in God's covenantal relationship with his creation, not of the exclusive nature of the believing community as in the Abrahamic covenant. If you begin with that point, thinking about the civic community as part of God's covenant of preserving grace—not redemptive but preserving—then it seems to me you are thinking very differently about civic community than if you fail to make that distinction between the body politic and the Church. The institutional question is primary. I think the whole question of common grace should at least have clued Calvin in to this. If natural law performed no other function for him, it should at least have raised a question in his mind about whether he was thinking in a biblically correct way about the civic community. If the basic purpose of the state is to maintain civil justice and order, and those things can be attained through the natural law, why then do we insist that the state ought to do something more?

Susan Schreiner: Don't forget the bondage of the will here. The fact that I know I should not cheat you in a contract does not mean that I have the ability to resist cheating you in a contract. The state, at least for Calvin, even without Christianity involved, has a coercive function that is very important. This coercive power is an integral part of why, above and beyond common grace, a magistrate is necessary. I think your comment on common grace is very important, that natural law really does concern a kind of common-grace theory in Calvin.

Luis Lugo: I want to press it further, because the question is not whether it is legitimate for government to coerce or not. Because of sin, government must coerce, as must, I may add, every other institution. Take families—I coerce my kids. If the Church has any sense of its own integrity, it should coerce people who blatantly dissent from its basic teachings. Coercion is part of the fallen human condition, whatever the institutional setting. The question is, coercion to what end? What is it appropriate for government to coerce people *to*? In what sphere is it legitimate for government to coerce? Calvin had not come to terms even biblically, never mind in terms of the natural law, with what is the appropriate sphere of governmental coercion. That's the problem here rather than the natural law vs. biblical law questions.

Susan Schreiner: I would say that Calvin would assume that the point or purpose of coercion by the civil magistrate is to preserve order, to preserve a living space for human beings. When he's dealing with a Christian magistrate, he thinks, as did everybody else, that this Christian magistrate is there to protect not only the bodies but also the souls of his constituency. If you want to get more grandiose about the Christian magistrate, in Calvin the purpose of all ordering institutions, coercive or not, is the glory of God. That's the final answer to everything.

Timothy George: Luis Lugo said that Calvin had not come to terms biblically with the appropriate sphere of governmental coercion. But what could he find in the Bible? There's not a lot in the New Testament about how to construct a civic community on Christian principles. What Calvin goes back to, and the Reformed tradition picks up on this, is this gender-blended term "nursing fathers." That's what a magistrate should be: a nursing father for the Church. Therefore, what is the goal of coercion, assuming the Christian magistracy? It is the establishment of the true worship of God and the support of the ministry of the Church for the preaching of the Gospel.

Keith Pavlischek: What the original Westminster Standards said about the authority of the civil magistrate is not all that different from what Calvin said. Both Calvin and the Westminster Confession recognized the institutional distinction between the civil magistrate and the authority of church elders. The civil magistrate, for instance, is not to administer the sacraments. So Calvin understood that there was an institutional separation.

But remember, the first table of the Decalogue, for Calvin as well as for Aquinas, is a part of the natural law. In other words, if you asked

Calvin and Thomas, "Should the civil magistrate enforce the requirements of natural law, and does that include placing restrictions on
violations of the first table, such as idolatry, within the bounds of
prudence?" they'd say, "Well, of course!" This raises the question of
what we say about Calvin and Thomas now. Do we want to say now,
in a different sociological context—i.e., under conditions of greater
social discord, lack of a common language, and so on—something
different than either Calvin or Thomas said? Do we change our
theology and say what they would not have said, that the first table of
the Decalogue is not a matter of natural law?

David Coffin: American Presbyterians did it at a time when there
was a consensus. Samuel Davies, Peck, Dabney—they argued in principle, at a time when there was a consensus, that it was wrong for the
magistrate to enforce the first table of the law. This was a principled
position, not growing out of the dissolution of Christendom and the
frustrations of the present age.

Russell Hittinger: The universal testimony of all the doctors of the
Church and the Reformers is that the first table of the Decalogue is
not only a matter of natural law but the very *essence* of the natural law
—just read *Veritatis Splendor*. All of the second table derives from it.
To deny, in principle (prudence is another matter), that the political
community cannot enforce the first table really raises doubts about
its ability to enforce the second, in my mind.

Paul Marshall: I'd like to go back to a basic point: that we don't
know what "natural" law means, or rather, it means a lot of quite
different things. I still think that the use of the term "natural" continues to provoke the sorts of problems we're dealing with. As an
adverb it's better, but there's still a problem of importing into the
discussion a concept that doesn't seem to have any Hebrew cognate.
Are we distinguishing *natural* from *divine,* which seems to be the
modern Catholic idea? Or is it *natural* v. *human,* which a lot of modern
natural law talk seems to be emphasizing? This would emphasize that
there are rules which we don't make up, which are given to us. That
sense of natural law is, I think, a fairly good sense. One of the ones
we are struggling with now is *natural* v. *revelatory.* Then you get

epistemological questions. Depending on what is being emphasized as "natural," very different sets of questions and answers come up.

David Smolin: I would like to bring us back to the problem of how we speak to the wider culture and in politics. It seemed to me that Russ Hittinger was saying in his paper that the Roman Catholic Church, in attempting to adapt to the modern political situation, particularly after World War II, made a move to embrace natural law as the means to do so. I think it's highly significant for Protestants if the current pope, whom I much admire, has found that, in carrying out this task, he has to revert back to Scripture and back to creation. That suggests that natural law cannot do everything that Catholics have wanted it to do. We have tried to make natural law do things that in earlier ages it did not have to do. It simply cannot carry that weight.

What do we put in its place? I want to point out that, at least in the American context, there is no lack of God-talk. We are dealing with two different levels of talk. On the academic level there is a distinct lack of God-talk. But in politics there is no lack of it, right, left, or center. The question becomes, on the political level, how God-talk is appropriately used. I think that the Pope is very insightfully trying to bring us back to those basic levels, to creation.

A big problem for Americans is the conjunction of God and "no, thou shalt not." This is true in our churches as much as in our political life. A rebellious human being or society can take any concept— natural law, natural rights, human rights, or even God—and twist it around to get the desired end result: that I can do what I want to do when I want to do it. No term is immune to this kind of abuse. In terms of God-talk, therefore, the problem is not simply how to get back to it, but how to see that it is appropriately used. In political discourse, in academic discourse, and in every other area of culture, we must talk about God—his creation, his providence, his rule—in a way that says unmistakably to human beings: You are not your own; there are limitations; there is a no.

Robert George: I have a couple of points to make, but first let me relate an incident from which I learned a lesson about God-talk and how usable it is. When I began my civil liberties course at Princeton last spring, I looked out at an audience of 250 very bright, enthusiastic undergraduates, and I began by quoting the words of the Declaration of Independence, "We hold these truths to be self-evident, that all men are created equal, that they are endowed by their Creator with certain unalienable rights, that among these are life, liberty, and the pursuit of happiness." I then said, "These are the foundational words of the American doctrine of civil liberties, and in light of the content of that doctrine as expressed in the Declaration, perhaps it wouldn't be inappropriate to begin our deliberations by offering thanksgiving to the Creator who endowed us with these rights. So let us in silence, each according to his own tradition and in his own way, give thanks to the Creator for our precious rights and liberties. Those of you who are not believers might take this opportunity to reflect in silence upon the source of our most important rights and liberties, which I believe you too cherish." I bowed my head for a solid minute—it seemed like an eternity—and when I glanced up there were 250 undergraduates with their heads bowed. Then I shot a glance over at seven or eight of my teaching assistants—graduate assistants and junior professors—and they were as white as ghosts. It was as if I were holding a gun on them. I guess they thought that the president of the university, or the ACLU, was going to come crashing in and arrest us. It was an amazing experience: there was one constituency in the room for whom God-talk made sense, but then there were the elites who were terrified at the very thought of it.

Now a couple of comments. First, I want to endorse Russ Hittinger's reminder that if there is a natural law, we have no options. We can choose to advert to it or not advert to it, to think about it or not think about it, to observe its principles or not observe its principles, but we can't choose to use it or not use it as if it were some sort of instrument. That would be like imagining that we could ask whether we should use language—we use language in the asking. I don't think Paul Marshall is right to say that we still haven't figured out what natural law is. I think we have questions about its content, about whether this principle or that principle is part of it. But for those of us who consider ourselves to be within the natural law tradition, I don't think we have a big dispute about whether it is a body of principles that provide reasons for action and are accessible to unaided reason. These principles are not the whole story of morality, but they're an important part of it.

Now I want to let the cat in amongst the pigeons, because my sense is that there really is a division, one that is important for the question of natural law. David Coffin spoke about the sense in which people could be involved in activities that constitute a this-worldly flourishing but nevertheless are not saving. I think this is the big one, because the relationship of this-worldly flourishing—achieved by acting in accordance with the principles of the natural law—to beatitude is something you have to decide one way or the other. In *Evangelium Vitae,* Pope John Paul II says right at the beginning,

> The church knows that this Gospel of Life, which she has received from her Lord, has a profound and persuasive echo in the heart of every person—believer and non-believer alike—because it marvelously fulfills all the heart's expectations while infinitely surpassing them. Even in the midst of difficulties and uncertainties, every person sincerely open to truth and goodness can, by the light of reason and the hidden action of grace, come to recognize in the natural law written in the heart the sacred value of human life from its very beginning until its end, and can affirm the right of every human being to have this primary good respected to the highest degree.

In a similar passage in *Veritatis Splendor,* which is concerned above all with the objectivity of moral truth—I wish I had it here so I could quote it precisely—the Pope says that in the moral life we have the way of salvation that is open even to those who do not know the Gospel. Someone who doesn't know the Gospel nevertheless has the way of salvation open to him in this world, and the way of salvation is the moral life.

Russell Hittinger: But the Pope also says "by . . . the hidden action of grace." The passage refers to what used to be called baptism of desire.

Robert George: Absolutely. This is not a "works" view that says you can do it without God's help at all. But if you don't know the Gospel, by acting on those principles in the heart of every person, believer or non-believer, "every person sincerely open to truth and goodness can, by the light of reason and the hidden action of grace . . ."

David Coffin: It seems to me that it is precisely this that causes Reformed theology to draw back from natural law. But I don't think that Reformed theology necessarily has to accept this interpretation. In what I said earlier I was suggesting a way of looking at natural law without seeing the possibility of salvation through the rational perception of goods blessed by grace. The introduction of the Pelagian principle is highly dangerous. It does seem to me that this is a critical point of difference between the two traditions.

Robert George: This is what I mean by letting the cat in amongst the pigeons.

Russell Hittinger: It's not a disjunction between grace and nature; it's two different doctrines of grace. I think Catholics have a different doctrine of grace, and it's not Pelagian. For instance, Pope John Paul II says, and here I quote, "Only in the ministry of Christ's redemption do we discover the concrete possibilities of man." Therefore it would be a serious error to conclude that the Church's teaching is only an ideal that must then be adapted, proportioned, graduated, to the so-called concrete possibilities of man. I think that the Catholic tradition has had a doctrine of grace, and not only of *gratias sanans,* repairing grace. Thomas says that God will not deny to any creature the grace to turn to him as savior.

William Edgar: I think maybe we have a difference in emphasis more than an absolute difference. Protestants, even in Reformed confessions, allow for the work of God's grace in ways exceptional to the norm. Now the norm is the preaching of the Gospel and a conscience response, but in the Westminster Confession, for example, there are two exceptions listed to that. One is for children who die in infancy. Now it's carefully said "elect" children who die in infancy, but it doesn't say who they are. Then it also has an exception for handicapped people—it doesn't use that language, but that's what's implied. I think that by opening up even that small door, Protestants will say there are ways that God can work outside the norm. They've been nervous, though, about speculating on this and building on it. I think that's where they perceive, in some Roman Catholics, too generous a view of how it could happen.

I was in a debate in Europe with a wonderful Dominican theologian about Christianity and world religions. He was making the point, which I don't think the Pope would share altogether, that people who have good will and are religiously inclined are actually on their way to the Church, whether they know it or not. He emphasized that it was because of Christ, it was because of grace. I leaned the other way and said, "But what about the corruption described in Romans 1?" In emphasis we were at two ends of a spectrum, but it wasn't a matter of saying it can only be this way or only that way.

David Coffin: Here's where my difficulty would arise. William Edgar mentioned that it is conceivable in the Reformed tradition that the Spirit, working where and when and how he will, would bring saving grace to a person quite apart from any act of faith or preaching of the Gospel. Let's acknowledge that as an abstract possibility, and in a couple of instances there seems to be biblical warrant for it— children dying in infancy, and so on. That's acknowledged as a possibility: a person saved through Christ, apart from any relation to the Gospel, by a sovereign act of God. Now here's the question: If you say there is a way of salvation open to one rationally seeking the good, via natural law, apart from the Gospel, is the same thing possible when the mind denies the good and rejects ordering the life according to beatitude? Is it still possible that God could, sovereignly by his grace, bring such a person to beatitude? If so, that's consistent with what I understand to be the nature of grace and the sovereignty of God. If not, if you assert only the former and not the latter, that is Pelagianism.

Robert George: I think we have a real difference here. I can't speak for Catholicism, and you can't speak for Calvinism, but I suspect that we're going to have behind us a lot of support within our traditions.

John West: But why is that so critical to natural law?

Robert George: There are two ways to approach this question. One is: What about babies who die? What about severely mentally handicapped people who are not leading the moral life because they are not involved in the moral game, they're not making moral choices?

And what about primitive peoples who haven't had the Gospel preached to them, or people before Christ came, and so on? But there's another way into the question, and that is, in general, through the relationship of this-worldly flourishing to heavenly beatitude. There should be some account given. Now, maybe the account that is preferable in the tradition will say, they aren't related. Or maybe the account will be one that instrumentalizes this-worldly flourishing to heavenly beatitude. There's a strand in the Catholic tradition—in my opinion a corrupt one, and I'm glad the Second Vatican Council got rid of it—that did treat this-worldly flourishing as merely instrumental to heavenly beatitude. That's what *Gaudium et Spes* overcomes by saying, no, it's not merely a means to an end; it's part of the end. So if you want to reject what I think is the Pope's position and the Catholic position, you should still develop some account that makes sense within the integrity of your whole view.

I'd like to go back to Calvin and ask Susan Schreiner a question. I was fascinated by her account of Calvin, and especially the quotations she marshalled for us, but it's not clear to me whether for Calvin the natural law, as it figures in human affairs, is fundamentally a matter of instinct, sentiment, feeling—a lot of the quotations use that language—or a matter of principles that are grasped intellectively and would therefore serve as reasons. If it's constituted by reasons, then a necessary condition of free choice is in place. If it's not, if instead it's constituted by feeling, sentiment, emotion, instinct, then I think a necessary condition of metaphysical freedom is not in place. And then I think it would be fair to say that if you secularize this view, if you drop God out of it, you get something very close to the Hobbesian/Humean understanding of the way people are constituted. That is, there very well might be a law of nature constituted by shared emotions or sentiments.

Susan Schreiner: The question is whether the unredeemed person understands the natural law with the intellective faculty or with the emotional faculty. Calvin's answer, I'm sorry to say, is: both. One reason it's both is that the conscience has a rational faculty and also a feeling faculty. The conscience can grasp the natural law in terms of reason, but it can also be confronted by natural law in a way that convicts, that shames. Calvin most often talks about the *rational* comprehension of natural law when he's talking about his admiration for the ancient jurists. When he's talking about the other, the *emotional* comprehension of natural law, he's usually talking about the horror of this or the horror of that—incest, adultery, even the pagans were ashamed, that sort of thing. But regarding the *rational* apprehension of principles of justice or natural law, he says in the *Institutes* that it's one thing for the human being to have a grasp of premises, but that the mind gets lost when it moves from premises to conclusions. That brings him back to his imagery of the mind as a labyrinth. One thing you have to keep in mind about Calvin is that, even when he is using intellective language about natural law, he is fundamentally Augustinian, as was Luther, in the diagnosis of human nature: our fundamental fracture is between knowing and doing.

Luis Lugo: This opens again the question of public discourse. If indeed the natural law functions at that deeper level, it is not sufficient to give rational reasons; one must also get at the gut, with the "in your heart you know we're right" sort of message. As academics we feel very uncomfortable with this, but it seems to me that appropriate Christian public discourse will incorporate both elements.

Carl Henry: Professor Schreiner said it is impossible to overestimate the power of sin on the human mind in the theology of the Reformers. In later comments she qualified that, but I want to speak to the initial comment. While it is true that corruption implicates the whole man, for Calvin the mind is less corrupted than the will. Man can no longer *do* good after the Fall, but he can *know* it—not necessarily all of it, but enough to condemn him in his revolt and rebellion.

Susan Schreiner: I will agree that Calvin says there are glimpses— I think he calls them lightning flashes—of truth that the mind can see. But I do think that Calvin is often presented as rationalistic in a way that he is not. Given his statements about the labyrinthine, slippery nature of the mind, the idolatrous nature of the mind—in an unredeemed perspective, the insights of the mind aren't going to do much for you besides condemn you. If your interest is in a public discourse that reaches out to those outside the faith, I think it's going to be problematic to put a lot of emphasis on persuasion.

Timothy George: I do agree with Dr. Henry that the will is more vitiated than the mind. But it's not much to brag about, partly, I think, because for Calvin, as for Augustine, human beings are essentially choosers and lovers. We are what we love. The will is, in a sense, more constitutive of human *qua* human than the mind.

Here's the quotation from the *Institutes* that Susan Schreiner was referring to, about the flashes of light. I think it's helpful. Calvin is talking about what we can know from nature, and he says, "They are like a traveler passing through a field at night, who in a momentary lightning flash sees far and wide, but the sight vanishes so swiftly that he is plunged again into the darkness of the night before he can even take a step, let alone be directed on his way by its help."

Joan O'Donovan: I've been concerned in both presentations of Calvin about the extent to which his doctrine of natural law is assimilated to a concept of order as imposition and restraint from the moment of creation. It seems to me that the relationship between law and love in the creation, which necessarily brings in a Christological element, has to be there somewhere. It's because of the dependence of Adam's original rectitude on the love of Christ and the grace of the Holy Spirit that we can address fallen mankind—whose conscience serves only to condemn and to induce violent feelings of guilt—and find a new starting point. The appeal to moral principles in the absence of an effort to bring lost humanity in touch with the foundation of Adam's rectitude may produce a minimum moral consensus that enables certain laws to be agreed upon and enforced. But it has really nothing to do with turning sinful humanity around to see where salvation is.

Luis Lugo: But there is a middle step there that you have left out. As I read Calvin, we must not confuse the language of bridling and restraining with the totality of what this grace outside the Gospel is about. There is a negative moment involved, to be sure, because the question is, how do you explain the fact that once we take the plunge into sin, we don't go all the way? There has to be something that restrains us from going all that way, so the accent there falls on the negative, on what restrains that sinful human impulse. But because that restraint is present, it opens up a human flourishing, for sin is not able to engulf all of God's good creation. A positive moment inevitably follows the negative, restraining, bridling sort of language.

Joan O'Donovan: But the positive moment has to be preceded as well. We've been presented with the continuity of restraint, which certainly is present in Calvin, from the restraining of the seas to the restraining of sinful human community. There is a continuity in Christ: Adam's original rectitude has been restored in Christ. It seems to me that this is where one begins in addressing the lost.

Susan Schreiner: But in Calvin there's nothing that is natural about that continuity. It is possible only because of predestination and the grace given to the predestined. There is no natural way to move from the sinfulness and fragmentation of human beings back toward a connection with the original Adam or a society run by the law of love. There is no way to get there by nature, whether it is natural reason or natural law.

Deal Hudson: I thought we came here to talk about good and evil, not heaven and hell. Something keeps pulling us toward consideration of ultimates, of eternity. What I'm still trying to get clear is whether or not we—both Protestants and Catholics—can agree that there is a third category available to us, whether we want to call it common ground or rational persuasion or whatever. We agree that this is probably the weakest of the three means available to us to have an impact on the *polis*. But if God calls us to love one another, it means we're supposed to love the whole of one another, meaning the whole life that we live. In loving one another we wish for one another the fullness of that life in the world, which means we wish, in a way—I don't mean this disrespectfully— more than salvation. We wish the good life, and all the goods of that life. This means that we address not just sinfulness but also privation, the lack of goods that we rationally accept as being necessary to a whole and good life. It seems to me, then, that we use all the weapons in our arsenal —evangelization, which is probably the most efficacious, coercion, properly understood, and rational persuasion.

David Coffin: There's a temptation to say, If you're really going to hold to the doctrine of total depravity—which certainly is integral, if anything is, to Calvinism—you don't have any hope for that third way; you've got to either evangelize or impose. Part of the significance of this discussion, and perhaps what the Calvinist can learn from the Roman Catholic tradition, is that, no, we're not left with just evangelism and imposition. But then the danger the Calvinist feels from the Catholic tradition is that you're going to introduce Pelagius into the mix and foul it all up. I think that's why this discussion, at least from my point of view, has been very fruitful.

Russell Hittinger: In the ancient Catholic ideal, which is certainly seen through the Middle Ages, the basic story is this: God wants his bride back. Adam and Eve are created to be, eventually, married to God, not just to each other. Thomas Aquinas himself says it is unthinkable that the first man did not know, by nature, that there would be an incarnation, because that's what human flourishing is all about. Hereafter, to flourish is to be wedded to God. This is the story of evangelization. When the Jesuit missionaries among the Hurons died one after another, they did it because they wanted to get God's bride back. That's true civilization-building. All of the Greek wisdom of our Catholic tradition in the Middle Ages was on the back of Cistercians, Benedictines, people who wanted to reconstitute nature as the bride of Christ. I would make a bid that that is not just evangelization but in a way is rational persuasion.

3

The Reformed Tradition and Natural Law

Daniel Westberg

In the late 1960s, partly as a reaction to the influence of situation ethics, some Protestant theologians began to speak of rehabilitating natural law.[1] Despite arguments that there was a definite natural law tradition in the Reformers, and that this could offer a base for a new Protestant understanding of the issue,[2] most Protestant ethicists or theologians have been wary of compromise with a doctrine of moral standards based on human nature or reason. And although there have been some friendly contacts in recent decades, Protestants continue to view with suspicion an approach that represents to them a deeply flawed tradition of Roman Catholic moral theology.

Helmut Thielicke's characterization of natural law "as conceived in the Aristotelian and Thomistic system" is representative:

Natural law is the law which belongs to man by nature, i.e., not by virtue of his bios but by virtue of what he essentially is. For this reason it is binding on all. It is independent of all outside influences,

Daniel Westberg is an assistant professor in the Department of Religious Studies at the University of Virginia, Charlottesville. He is the author of *Right Practical Reason: Aristotle, Action, and Prudence in Aquinas* (Clarendon Press, 1994).

including those of existent positive laws. Indeed, so far from being
influenced by those laws it is itself normative for them. It is
grounded in the relatively undisturbed likeness between creator
and creature. Finally, it can be known by all, and thus constitutes
a norm to which all are accountable "by nature."[3]

Written before Vatican II, this exaggerates and slants some issues. Yet
it represents a standard line of criticism that may be summarized as
follows: (1) the basis of natural law theory in a nonbiblical and archaic
metaphysics, (2) the over-reliance on reason, (3) the minimizing of
the doctrine of original sin, (4) the static view of human nature, (5) the
tendency to assume universal norms from projected particular cultural
norms, and (6) the assumption of the authority to define and teach
by the Roman Catholic Church.

The objections to natural law are usually directed against Catholic
presentations. This is partly because the Catholic tradition is a live
(though changing) one; it aims at some consistency and faithfulness,
and it also fits into Protestant polemics against nature, grace, and
casuistry. So Catholic natural law doctrine is a handy target. But this
posture also reflects an ignorance of the legacy of natural law in
Protestantism. In fact, the errors and exaggerated claims for natural
law that arose in later *Protestant* versions explain in part its demise
and the suspicion that remains. The danger for Protestant moral
theory has been, not so much that Presbyterian parsons might be
seduced by the *De legibus* of Aquinas's *Summa* by reading it on the
sly, but that, in the absence of consistent principles and a sound
tradition of treatment, there has been an idiosyncratic development
with inappropriate claims. This has brought discredit on the whole
enterprise.

On the whole, the Reformed tradition has been moderate in its
stance: not as categorically opposed as some strains of Lutheranism,
able at times to use the Scholastic tradition, but retaining more suspicion and distance than the kind of Anglicanism represented by
Richard Hooker.[4]

I propose to discuss several theologians who fall broadly within the
Reformed tradition of theology: Heinrich Bullinger, William Ames,
Hugo Grotius, and Emil Brunner. This will require some considera-
tion of the way I read Calvin's theory in order to set the stage for the

later tradition, but my survey of Calvin will be restricted to a sketch of a few important themes.

One purpose of this paper is simply to present the lines of development within an important Protestant tradition; but a second is to shed light on those problem areas, such as rationalism and original sin, that require more specific targeting if we are to concede that Calvin is sound on sin, yet still has a doctrine of natural law. I also hope that a look at some weaknesses of the later Protestant versions will be of service to those who agree with the possibility of a non-Catholic natural law doctrine.

JOHN CALVIN (1509-1564)

Calvin's doctrine of natural law has received mixed reviews. The reason, in part, is that, in comparison to both medieval and later versions, it is guarded and restrained and thus tends toward minimalism, and in part, that some readers of Calvin have not distinguished the different purposes of natural law doctrine nor recognized the context of the different discussions. For our purposes here, three points may be made.

First, natural law for Calvin seems primarily to be a means of affirming the presence of a universal moral standard, a guide for conscience in a most general way, a guide that the reality of sin prevents us from following very well. Calvin's fundamental concern, in line with Romans 2, is the justice of God's judgment:

> The purpose of natural law, therefore, is to render man inexcusable. This would not be a bad definition: natural law is that apprehension of the conscience which distinguishes sufficiently between just and unjust, and which deprives men of the excuse of ignorance, while it proves them guilty by their own testimony.[5]

Calvin's commentary on Romans 2:15 corroborates this: what human beings have is not the power to _fulfill_ the law but the _knowledge_ of it; even there, it is a case of having just enough knowledge of the law— "only some seeds of what is right implanted in their nature"—to be held responsible.[6] What can be relied on from this vestigial amount of God's law is minimal: while the conscience is a kind of "inner witness" of what a person owes to God, that person is "so shrouded in the darkness of errors that he hardly begins to grasp through this natural law what worship is acceptable to God."[7] That is why revelation was so essential: ". . . the Lord has provided us with a written law to give us a clearer witness of what was too obscure in the natural law, shake off our listlessness, and strike more vigorously our mind and memory."[8]

A second point is that natural law does provide some basis for an objective moral order. This is mainly taught in the last section of the *Institutes:*

> The moral law . . . is contained under two heads, one of which simply commands us to worship God with pure faith and piety; the other, to embrace men with sincere affection. Accordingly, it is the true and eternal rule of righteousness, prescribed for men of all nations and times, who wish to conform their lives to God's will. For it is his eternal and unchangeable will that he himself indeed be worshiped by us all, and that we love one another.[9]

Calvin was aware, as Aquinas was, that some societies or cultures have had laws that violated primary principles of natural law:

> For I do not think that those barbarous and savage laws such as gave honor to thieves, permitted promiscuous intercourse, and others both more filthy and more absurd, are to be regarded as laws. For they are abhorrent not only to all justice, but also to all humanity and gentleness.[10]

This does not undermine such a version of natural law, because it does not claim that all societies clearly recognize the norms. Even this assessment is an indirect indication of these standards, however, because it is by the standard of justice, or principles of humanity and gentleness, that we consider such societies defective.

A third point to be made about Calvin's view of natural law is that the principles that can be assigned to natural law are extremely general. Because individuals and societies do not inherently have a clear set of principles, they can easily be mistaken. And countries will structure and formulate their legal systems in a wide variety of ways. Yet these laws "must be in conformity to that perpetual rule of love, so that they indeed vary in form but have the same purpose."[11]

An example of the validity of natural law at a very general level, one in which Calvin shows a difference from many later thinkers, is in his discussion about the diversity of punishments possible. Stealing is forbidden by God's law, but punishments have varied from flogging through double restitution to exile or even death. All laws tend to the same end—punishment for those crimes that God's law condemns —but they do not agree on the manner of punishment. Certain societies have more problems with particular vices, so it follows that they have to deal more harshly than others with thieves, say, or murderers, or they will be threatened by chaos. Calvin shares the wisdom of Aquinas in refusing to identify capital punishment for murder as something demanded by natural law.[12]

HEINRICH BULLINGER (1504-1575)

Bullinger was a near contemporary of Calvin, a colleague and successor to Zwingli at Zurich. He was one of the most ecumenically minded of the Reformers, pursuing discussions with Calvin and the Lutherans, and he substantially contributed to the articulation of Reformed theology in his drafting of the Second Helvetic Confession (1566). Possibly from disposition, and from his search for common areas of agreement, Bullinger was more favorably disposed toward natural law than was Zwingli.[13] In a sermon on Romans 2 Bullinger wrote:

The law of nature is an instruction of the conscience, and as it were, a certain direction placed by God himself in the minds and hearts of men, to teach them what they have to do and what to eschew. And the conscience, verily, is the knowledge, judgment and reason of a man. . . .[14]

No less than Calvin, Bullinger had a healthy regard for the corrosive effects on knowledge of human sinfulness:

But the disposition of mankind being flatly corrupted by sin, as it is blind so also is it in all points evil and naughty. It knoweth not God, it worshippeth not God, neither doth it love the neighbour; but rather is affected with self-love toward itself, and seeketh still for its own advantage. For which cause the apostle said, "that we by nature are the children of wrath." Wherefore the law of nature

> [is so called] . . . because God hath imprinted or engraven in our minds some knowledge, and certain general principles of religion, justice, and goodness, which because they be grafted in us and born together with us, do therefore seem to be naturally in us.[15]

Bullinger seems in line with Calvin on original sin, on the tendency toward self-love, and on natural law's functioning not as a reliable guide but as an indicator of general principles. After enumerating the ways in which pagans have some recognition of the moral law (e.g., respect for parents, regard for truth, laws against theft and murder), Bullinger writes:

> So then by all this we may easily gather, that even in the Gentiles' minds also were graven a certain knowledge of God, and some precepts whereby they knew what to desire, and what to eschew; which notwithstanding they did corrupt, and make somewhat misty, with the evil affections and corrupt judgments of the flesh.[16]

In a way similar to Calvin's, Bullinger summarized the main intention of the natural law as involving two points: (1) to acknowledge God, and worship him, and (2) to keep or maintain society and friendship among men. The first is based on Romans 1:19-21—God's power and deity can be "clearly perceived in the things that have been made"—while the second is based on the teaching of Jesus in Matthew 7 that whatever you would like others to do to you, you should do to them. Differences from Calvin emerge here, because Bullinger's appeal to the golden rule is not the same as Calvin's assertion that love is the aim of the law. There is also significance in Bullinger's addition of specifications of the general rule: "Moreover, to that general law belong these that follow: Live honestly: hurt not another; give every man his own; provide things necessary for life, and keep it from distress."[17]

Bullinger had a confidence in unchanging norms or moral absolutes that places his doctrine beyond Calvin's:

> Among all men, at all times and of all ages, the meaning and substance of the laws touching honesty, justice, and public peace, is kept inviolable: if change be made, it is circumstances, and the law is interpreted as the case requireth, according to justice and a good end.[18]

An indication of what is happening here, the appeal to an objective moral order to ground more contingent convictions, is provided by Bullinger's statement about murder in his sermon on the sixth commandment:

> The law saith, "Let no man kill another: let him that killeth another be killed himself." That law remaineth for ever unchangeable, neither is it lawful for any man at any time to put it out or wipe it away.[19]

Bullinger's interpretation makes retributive punishment a requirement of natural law rather than a disposition of positive law.

Although he recognizes the distortion of reason by sin, and the possibilities of cultural ignorance, Bullinger nevertheless is moving us in the direction of a larger content, more specificity, and indeed absoluteness, in the group of natural law principles. He also implies, at least in the sermon on the sixth commandment, that highly specific civil laws are a useful means of promoting moral virtue.[20]

WILLIAM AMES (1576-1633)

Ames was a convinced and conservative Puritan; he refused to accommodate himself to Anglican authorities and spent the last third of his life in exile in the Netherlands, where he came to be a major influence in the theology of English, Dutch, and American Puritanism.[21] In writing *Conscience and the Cases Thereof*, meant to be a Protestant answer to Roman Catholic casuistry, Ames did not hesitate to make use of the treatment of Aquinas, but his independent attitude and the differences that emerge show him to be removed from Richard Hooker's approach.

Hooker was more deferential to the authority of Aquinas, since he found the Thomistic view of law and moral principles useful against the arguments of some Puritans in favor of a purely biblical standard. The picture of an orderly universe, governed by a system of laws essentially rational and accessible to the human mind, is emphasized by Hooker so strongly, however, that his approach goes beyond Aquinas and has more in common with the views of Francis Bacon.[22]

For Ames, natural law is linked with God's governance of the universe. From God's perspective this is the eternal Law, the principles of God's direction; but from a human perspective it is natural, "as it is ingrafted and imprinted in the Nature of man by the God of Nature."[23] Ames showed his familiarity with the Scholastic tradition by treating the question of the epistemology of natural law under the heading *synteresis,* defined as the apprehension of the Law of Nature. Greatly enlarging its scope (compared, say, to Aquinas), Ames refers to it as "not onely generall conclusions touching right or Law, which are deduced by good consequence out of naturall principles, but likewise all practicall truths, whereunto wee give a firme assent, through the revelation wee have by faith."[24] It is hard to avoid the conclusion that Ames had a somewhat Platonic view of innate moral principles.[25]

Ames certainly took into account the reality of original sin and the effects of the Fall, which is why the moral law had to be promulgated and restored by revelation:

> But ever since the corruption of our Nature, such is the blindnesse of our understanding and perversenesse of our will and disorder of our affections that there are only some Reliques of that Law remaining in our hearts like to some dimme aged picture, and therefore by the voyce and power of God it ought to bee renewed as with a fresh pencill. Therefore is there no where found any true right practicall reason, pure and complete in all parts, but in the written Law of God.[26]

Ames was concerned with the relation between moral law and natural law, and discussed three general precepts: (1) to live honestly, (2) not to hurt another, and (3) to give each his due. These are not wholly adequate, because the worship of God is omitted, and the others require more specification.[27] The golden rule is a precept both natural and divine, not equivalent to the whole of natural law, but summing up the area involving relations with others.

Ames posed a question about the relation of the Mosaic law to natural law. All the precepts of the Decalogue except the fourth (it is interesting that most of the Christian tradition did not see keeping the sabbath as rooted in the doctrine of creation) are part of natural law, for these reasons: (1) there is nothing in them not applicable to all nations; (2) there is nothing that is not necessary to human nature; (3) there is nothing that is not grounded on right reason; (4) these principles are approved "even of the more understanding sort of the Heathen"; (5) all conduce to the benefit of mankind in this present life.[28]

There is some tension in Ames's treatment between the emphasis put on the knowledge of moral principles, the recognition of the effects of sin, and the need for revelation. For instance, Ames makes a higher claim for the innate knowledge of certain principles than did Aquinas, who emphasized the role of experience; and Ames is similar to Calvin in emphasizing the need for revelation in view of the vestigial remains of the image after the Fall. Nevertheless, with the Decalogue as the centerpiece Ames is able to provide a basis for a common morality in society and among nations.

HUGO GROTIUS (1583-1645)

Grotius was a child prodigy, matriculating at the University of Leiden at the age of eleven. Trained in law and theology, he took the side of Arminius in the Calvinist controversies of the seventeenth century, was arrested and confined, but escaped to France. He was an internationalist in his ecumenical interests as well as in his concern for the law of nations.

Grotius's *De iure belli ac pacis* has been highly influential, leading some to proclaim him the father of international law. His theory of natural law is presented mainly in the prolegomena and first book, where he provides this definition:

> The law of nature is a dictate of right reason, which points out that an act, according as it is or is not in conformity with rational [and social] nature, has in it a quality of moral baseness or moral necessity; and that, in consequence, such an act is either forbidden or enjoined by the author of nature, God.[29]

The bracketed words "and social" were in the original but were somehow missing from Kelsey's 1925 translation and also from the Latin text used as the basis.[30] However, the social dimension of human society was acknowledged by Grotius, and fundamental to his view:

> But among the traits characteristic of man is an impelling desire for society, that is, for the social life—not of any and every sort,

but peaceful, and organized according to the measure of his intelligence, with those who are of his own kind; this social trend the Stoics called "sociableness." Stated as a universal truth, therefore, the assertion that every animal is impelled by nature to seek only its own good cannot be conceded.[31]

This is not so far from Calvin's understanding of the function of natural law in society, but Grotius expresses a confidence that Calvin did not have in positive qualities of human nature. Grotius believes that in children, for example, even before their training has begun, "some disposition to do good to others appears," and "sympathy for others comes out spontaneously."[32] Readers concerned with the Reformers' view of original sin will note the contrast between Grotius and St. Augustine's observations in the *Confessions* on the nature of children.

Not only does natural law stem from our need and desire to maintain the social order, but Grotius thought he could then deduce these principles of social order: (1) abstinence from that which is another's, (2) restoration to another of anything of his that we may have (together with any gain we may have received), (3) the obligation to fulfill promises, (4) restitution for a loss incurred through our fault, and (5) the inflicting of penalties upon men according to their deserts.[33]

There is some controversy about the interpretation of Grotius's statement *etiamsi daremus non esse Deum*—even if we should concede that there is no God, these principles would still be valid. It seems to be a reversion to a Stoic view, or the rejection of the theological basis for natural law, and many consider this a sign of the development towards a modern secularist view of law. This may, strictly speaking, be unfair to Grotius, who continued to affirm the importance of a theological grounding both for the authority of natural law and for a proper understanding of justice.[34] It may well be that what Grotius was denying was the contention that the moral law is connected purely to the arbitrary will of God (as in the voluntarism of Occam and late Scholastics), and that he was seeking to affirm the importance of an objective order of reality as a moral basis.

The uneasiness that people have with Grotius may develop not so much at a foundational level, where there is a divorce of natural law from theology, but at the practical level, where there is little recognition of either the need for illumination to counteract sin-induced blindness, the importance of wisdom, or the value of revelation in bringing clarity and certainty (as in Aquinas). Thus the problem is that God is important to Grotius as foundation or guarantor, a position that tends towards deism.

The problematic aspect of rationalism in Grotius is his confidence in the clarity of certain foundational principles, and in the human ability to construct a system from them. This kind of rationalism is what moves Grotius away from the Scholastics and from the previous reformed tradition. He claims that:

> For the principles of that law, if only you pay strict heed to them, are in themselves manifest and clear, almost as evident as are those things which we perceived by the external sense; and the senses do not err if the organs of perception are properly formed. . . .[35]

Kilner criticizes Grotius for expecting people to be able to "pay strict heed," and says that his notion of right reason "is seriously jeopardized in most if not all people."[36] Although there is a legitimate question about Grotius's view of the effects of sin, this is somewhat off the mark here in respect to the function of natural law, because Grotius, like Calvin, would distinguish between the knowledge people have of what to do and their ability to perform it.

Still, if we refine or better focus this critique, and compare Grotius with Aquinas or Calvin, there is a confidence about the possibility of constructing a whole system of natural law that is something new. The older tradition emphasized certain points that tended to limit the tendency to universal systematizing: (1) there is uncertainty of application in different conditions; (2) the element of self-evidence applies only to the first principles, and does not imply universal knowledge; (3) the more one moves from general principle to particular principles, the more uncertainty there is; and (4) the influence of passion and bad habits can obscure the knowledge of natural law in both individuals and societies. A practical result of this difference is that where the Scholastics only talked about the general institutions of marriage, family, and property as being part of natural law, in Grotius the specific institutions familiar to him had that status.[37]

For Calvin, the knowledge of principles was affected by sin; for

114   DANIEL WESTBERG

Bullinger, natural law was "misty"; and for Ames, what remained to us were bits of a "dim aged picture." Grotius, however, partly because it suited his agenda to imply universal agreement for his principles, and partly because he had shifted from the convictions of Reformed theology about the effects of sin and selfishness, claimed much more for the clarity of his principles than Aquinas or Calvin did for theirs.

EMIL BRUNNER (1889-1966)

Brunner discusses autonomy, natural law, and love in his influential work on ethics, *The Divine Imperative.* There can be no fixed or absolute sense of right in all human beings, because that is based on a Stoic view of abstract equality. From the Christian perspective of creation, the chief concern of the law is the preservation of life within the realm of sin; the law is not concerned to win the realm of sin for the realm of redemption.[38]

> The creative purpose of God, determined by His redemptive purpose, is—not the norm, but the *point of view* for the discovery of the best possible form of law. The other point of view is that of existing reality. The same is true of the other forms of civilization in so far as they come under the ethical point of view. This, and not a principle, we might describe as the idea of a *Christian Natural Law.*[39]

Brunner attempted to clarify the confusions about natural law in an extensive footnote in which he distinguishes between relative and absolute—absolute natural law reflects the original created order, while relative natural law takes into account the Fall and the limitations and corruption of human nature. Brunner objects to presentations of Catholic social ethics that give the impression of absolute natural law and unchanging moral norms:

> Were the contrast between the absolute and relative Law of Nature openly admitted and carried into practice, at once it would be seen that the relative Law of Nature is *not* a *law* at all, but only a *regulative principle,* from which no definite demands can be deduced, but all that it determines is this: that in the sinful world, so far as possible the absolute Law of Nature must be carried out.[40]

Like Jacques Maritain and so many others, Brunner was moved by the experience of World War II to reevaluate social principles and incorporate a new view of natural law. He wrote *Justice and the Social Order* in Zurich in the middle of the war, and at the conclusion of a significant chapter on natural law he said, ". . . the totalitarian state, which arose on the ruins of the law of nature, has been the means of bringing it to life again."[41] The treatment marks a departure from his earlier discussion. Gone is the distinction between relative and absolute; and the essence of natural law is seen as justice, not self-preservation.

Brunner identified three types of natural law: the pre-Christian, the modern (descended from Grotius), and the Christian view, in which "nature is the divine creative ordinance of God, of the God who revealed his will to mankind in Jesus Christ."[42] When modern thinkers reject natural law, it is usually the modern tradition that they reject; they are likely to be unfamiliar with the classical or Christian traditions. What Christians mean by "law of nature" is simply and solely the order of creation.[43] Common to all three types of natural law is the affirmation of "a justice which transcends human caprice and convention, a principle which is a valid standard of sacred authority." The classical definition of justice becomes the essential element: "Whoever admits the *suum cuique* ["to each his due"] has in principle admitted the law of nature."[44]

Although Brunner profited from a reappraisal of the Reformation doctrine of sin (as did Reinhold Niebuhr), there is little evidence that he based his later approach on a fresh reading of Calvin on natural law. Evidence that he did not is seen in his transformation of natural law into natural rights, and in his espousal of the centrality of justice, interpreted as "to each his due." The order of creation is important to establish human rights as inherently given by God:

> The rights of communities are rights which go back to a relationship between men based on the order of creation—for instance, that of man and woman in marriage. In the last resort all justice means these constants of creation as a basis on which every human being receives his due.[45]

> For in the Christian doctrine of justice, the principle of inalienable rights of the individual human being is blended with that of mem-

bership of a social body; not only the equal dignity of men, but also their natural inequality and the fellowship of completion based on it, are derived from God's creation. If the idea of justice had remained faithful to its Christian form, to the Christian theory of the law of nature, the great breach in the development of law and the state would not have been necessary.[46]

Brunner's summary of Christian justice and his attempt to correct misconceptions of it point back somewhat to the social element of the traditional conception, but they do not really bring us very close to Calvin's theological view.

Concluding Observations

From Calvin to Grotius, the following lines of development may be noted:

1. Vague general principles gradually became more specific formulations as part of the content of natural law. Where Calvin allowed punishment in general as part of natural law, Bullinger and others identified capital punishment itself as part of the law of nature. Also notable is an increasing confidence in the absoluteness and clarity of the main principles of natural law.

2. Awareness of the effects of original sin remains stronger in the tradition through Bullinger and Ames, but with Grotius it becomes weak. Though partly related to his rejection of conservative Calvinism, this weakening also reflects the general prevalence of more favorable assessments of human nature.

3. The foundation of natural law in the sociability of human nature, though tied to a somewhat optimistic view of human nature in Grotius, is not in itself a sign of distortion of the tradition, because Calvin certainly emphasized the social dimension of natural law. In the doctrine of the German legal philosopher Samuel Pufendorf (1632-1694), however, sociability takes on the status of an Archimedean point completely removed from revelation.

4. Perhaps the chief and fatal characteristic of the later natural law presentations is the feature of deductivism. This is the assumption that from a few clear and certain principles one can rationally deduce a set of moral principles and convert them to civic laws, thus claiming

for the legal system a grounding in natural law. This is manifest in Grotius (and even more so in Pufendorf); hints of it are found as early as Bullinger, less so in Ames, and not at all in Calvin. It is this feature that separates the early modern theories from the Scholastic and Reformation versions of natural law. The decisive twentieth-century rejection of naturalism in moral philosophy and in theology by both liberals and fundamentalists[47] becomes more understandable when seen as a reaction to the kind of ethics represented by the assumption of rational systems, both Catholic and Protestant.

Brunner's difficulties in debating natural theology with Karl Barth, his own sense of distance from Calvin's discussion of natural law, and the shift in political discussion from natural law to natural rights all make one wonder whether the tradition can be revived. But given the fresh reappraisals in Catholic circles and the keen interest among a number of Protestants, this may indeed be an opportune time for a new consideration of the important tradition of natural law.

A Response

William Edgar

Many Protestants who have been hibernating in Karl Barth's winter are ready for a spring thaw. In the earlier part of the twentieth century, rightly concerned over the older liberalism's confidence in the capacities of reason, they could see no place for even a humbler sort of natural theology. Today they are beginning to think there may be something to it. This is no doubt in response to the challenge of a society overly concerned about rights, a concept that is a secularization of natural law. But the new interest is also a result of stimulating contacts with Roman Catholic thinkers, who stand in a more consistent tradition than we.

If we Protestants hope to restore proper thinking about natural law, and especially if we aim to use such thinking for credible public discourse, much more work is needed. The first step is indeed to look at our tradition, and for this task Daniel Westberg's paper serves us well. Westberg is concerned about possible weaknesses in Protestant moral theory owing to its unsystematic treatment of the questions raised by natural law. Because of their tendency to throw out the baby with the bath water, Protestants have not benefited from the enterprise as much as they could. As a step toward correcting this deficiency, Westberg sumarizes the history of Protestant discussion by offering succinct, accurate snapshots of five of its major figures, and then shows its fate.

John Calvin's threefold teaching on natural law has been the crux

---

William Edgar is a professor of apologetics at Westminster Theological Seminary, Philadelphia, and also a *professeur associé* at the Faculté Libre de Théologie Réformée in Aix-en-Provence, France. He is an ordained minister in the Presbyterian Church in America.

118

of further developments. First, the Reformer affirms that the basic thrust of natural law is to defend mankind's knowledge of God and mankind's inability to process that knowledge correctly. God's general revelation does indeed reach every person; when God is denied, it is not because of lack of clarity in the revelation but because of a moral refusal to comply with the truth. The second theme in Calvin, in fact, is that the world's many societies all show they have received natural law, at least in some measure. Love is the basic principle at its heart. Accordingly, societies display respect for certain norms flowing from love, such as humanity and righteousness, though they surely do so in a flawed manner. But third, and most important for our purposes, Calvin fully recognized that, although the principles of the revealed law do not vary, their applications do. Different punishments for the same crimes can be envisaged because of the very different characteristics exhibited from one country to another. In our time we might call these cultural variants.

In Protestant discussions following Calvin, neither the centrality of love nor the flexibility of application has been consistently expounded. Already with Bullinger, natural law is more related to justice than to love, and correctly applying natural law makes it requisite always to have certain punishments for certain crimes. In the post-Reformation Protestants, a trend toward seeing natural law as compelling and universal sets in. William Ames, for example, in order to answer the casuists, considered natural law to be ingrafted in the world and in human nature. He expanded the breadth of natural law to the point that it becomes a basis for universal moral law. He saw the law of God, especially the Decalogue, as the centerpiece of common morality. He did recognize the limiting power of sin, but thought that this only tempered the possibility of finding a common framework for morality.

Along with many historians, Westberg makes it clear that a crucial shift occurred with Hugo Grotius. Not only did Grotius have a higher view of the reliability of reason than his predecessors, but he also held to a somewhat mechanistic universe. Westberg cites the saying attributed to Grotius, that principles of natural law would still be valid were there no God.[1] And he correctly points out that the real concern of Grotius's readers was not so much his uncoupling of natural law from theology as his trust in unaided reason. Furthermore, it may not be entirely fair to lay the blame for secularization on Grotius. Westberg points out that it was thinkers like Pufendorf who pushed natural law over the line and ushered in deism. The stage is then set for David Hume's division between *is* and *ought,* and then, in our own times, for G. E. Moore's so-called naturalistic fallacy.

For further reflection I suggest we explore two avenues. The first is to take a closer look at the reasons for the shift Westberg has described. Tracking the shift from Calvin to Hume and Moore requires far more historical work than can be done in a brief paper, of course. It is work well worth undertaking. This could be most valuable for Christians hoping to find a language of public discourse that has some authority. Finding out exactly how the secularization of natural law occurred is the first step toward recovering whatever value there may be to the tradition. The second thing I would like to do here is to take another look at what the biblical data say about natural law. Not only is this the necessary complement of a critical diagnosis, but it is the only basis for ethics that can claim ultimacy.

TRACING THE SECULARIZATION

Mapping out a massive shift such as the secularization of natural law requires paying some attention to the social setting. Though one could find roots in the Middle Ages, certainly the pivotal point is the seventeenth century. In 1648 the Peace of Westphalia not only signaled the end of the major European wars of religion but also laid the groundwork for the modern nation. The sovereign state gained an unprecedented autonomy, which fed into the social pluralism connected with modernity. The need to establish criteria for civil discourse in a pluralistic context was an important factor behind the attempt to tone down the peculiarities of the Christian message and look for more universal principles.

In this social setting, dramatic shifts began to occur in the history of ideas. Science gained a new impetus in the seventeenth century, and the relationship between science and religion became a major subject for Christian apologetics. Desirous of showing how God's purposes were demonstrated in nature, many apologists moved from Calvin's position to a more mechanistic worldview.

Consider Francis Bacon, who taught there were two books, Scripture and nature. The two were to be "read" as two kinds of revelation carrying the same message. Or consider Walter Charleton, who in *Darkness of Atheism* (London, 1752) went to great lengths to prove the wisdom of the God who set into nature a "commodious disposition of the parts" where everything makes sense. Accordingly, the sun is neither too close nor too far away. If it were closer, we would burn up; if farther, we would freeze. In every detail God's care is imbedded in nature, so that his providence is clearly perceptible to the human conscience. Or consider John Ray, who proclaimed that everything God has made is for a purpose, and that all created things display God's power and wisdom. In his popular *The Wisdom of God Manifested in the Works of Creation* (London, 1691) Ray refuted Descartes, who had objected to the idea that human observers could always tell God's purposes. In many things, Ray affirmed, the divine purpose is so clear that we do not need the help of theology to discern it. For example, the eye is so obviously for seeing that we may praise God for it without needing to know more about how it may have been created.

One of the most forthright and prolific of these "virtuosi" of the seventeenth century is Robert Boyle. In *Usefulness of Experimental Philosophy* (London, 1668) he argued that a proper analysis of the works of God in nature should uncover a proper view both of the Creator and of human ethics. Here and in his other writings Boyle averred that nature vindicates God's glory in two ways: first as his agent to carry out his purposes, and second as the setting for divine intrusions. Whenever the purposes of God cannot be directly accomplished through autonomous nature, God must and will intervene. Providence becomes a matter of either accommodating whatever laws are set in place, or intruding in order to assert a special purpose. It is as though the law of inertia had defined the way in which divine wisdom could be manifested.

Following this line, Christian apologists argued for God's truth by analogy with the patterns in nature. For example, some theologians sought to prove the immortality of the soul by appealing to the continuity of the soul throughout the human life cycle. Since the soul was the same in infancy, adulthood, and old age, despite change in the form of the body, why should death prevent the soul from existing into eternity? This kind of argument made sense to an audience that believed in the law of inertia. What was happening toward the end of the seventeenth and the beginning of the eighteenth century was that nature's laws were becoming more and more predictable. They were understood to reveal God's goodness more and more clearly. Natural law was no longer obscured by the noetic effects of sin in the observer. Instead, natural law was the unobstructed conduit of God's wisdom. When there were unexplained providences, such as storms or disease, God was taken to be their author, but he acted by intruding into, rather than accommodating, the laws of nature. Nevertheless, the laws were intact.[2]

Post-Reformation Orthodox Views

Deism began to replace orthodox Christianity in the seventeenth century, and the natural world was increasingly considered independent from the complex, enigmatic guidance of God. In a word, nature was becoming autonomous. Were there voices to the contrary? The tradition that has come to be called post-Reformation orthodoxy, or, less happily, Protestant scholasticism, strongly denied any idea that natural law provided a foundation for true philosophy. Neither in the early era after Calvin, represented by Pierre Du Moulin and Lambert Daneau, nor in the high orthodox era, with Herman Witsius and François Turretin, is there any concession to rationalism. To be sure, the post-Reformation Protestants did not all share this emerging philosophy of secular natural law.

Perhaps the most influential post-Reformation Protestant of the seventeenth century was François Turretin (1623-1687). In the section on natural theology in his classic work *The Institutes,* he affirms two things about natural law.[3] First, there is valid revelation outside Scripture. Turretin says, "We find in man a natural law written upon each one's conscience excusing and accusing them in good and bad actions, which therefore necessarily implies the knowledge of God, the legislator, by whose authority it binds men to obedience and proposes rewards or punishments" (I.iii.5). He enumerates various evidences for the reality of natural law. Among them are the clear manifestations of the sense of deity in every nation, even the most barbarous, so that a certain natural theology can be undertaken. To be sure, such knowledge of God varies in degree, but it is real and useful in all societies. Second, Turretin considers natural theology unable to lead to salvation. This is because Christ is revealed only in the Gospel, not in nature. Furthermore, the knowledge men have of God because of natural law is partial, imperfect, corrupt, and obscure (III.iv.6). It is sufficient to render us inexcusable but not to save us (III.iv.9).

In general, Turretin represents the mainstream of the post-Reformation Protestant view of natural law. Theologians differed in emphases, some considering philosophy a form of natural theology, others using the term only for what can be deduced from the conscience. But always a sharp difference was affirmed between natural and supernatural knowledge. According to Richard A. Muller's excellent study, the distinction is so sharp that the claim that the orthodox allowed for supernatural theology to be built on natural revelation is "utterly erroneous."[4]

Drifting Toward Moralism

What eventually did happen in Protestant circles was a drift toward moralism. The orthodox tradition was not able to resist the ascendancy of the Enlightenment worldview. Many theologians, wanting to defend Christianity, moved from believing that morality needed to come exclusively from on high, to the view that there were timeless codes shared by most great civilizations, codes that could be discovered by unaided reason. G. W. Leibniz (1646-1716), who had an enormous influence, taught that though faith is superior to reason, there is no real conflict between the two. His disciple Christian Wolff (1679-1754) believed that the law of non-contradiction was universal, and that truth, whether revealed or not, was a philosophical necessity. Jacob Vernet (1698-1789) and Jean-Alphonse Turretin, the son of François, taught that true religion always fits human needs and aspirations.[5] The Scottish school of Common Sense Realism, spearheaded by Thomas Reid (1710-1796), attacked skepticism by positing direct knowledge of things, based on reason plus sense perception.

In this climate, not only did the source of morality change, but its content changed as well. Moral rules that did not appear to jibe with common sense were considered dubious. Furthermore, the notion of God himself was modified, from one who deserves praise however mysterious his ways may appear, to one who is basically a reasonable moral agent.[6] To use the apt metaphors of W. R. Everdell, Christianity moved from being a "bridle" by which men are restrained to being a "spring" that is the source of moral behavior in all people.[7]

From this shift the next steps were predictable: a belief in progress, in the ability of criticism to solve any number of problems—in short, secularization. Natural law for Calvin had been indissolubly connected to God's authority, and was fallibly interpreted by sinful human beings. By the nineteenth century, natural law had become a semi-autonomous principle perceivable by unaided reason. Christianity had drifted from being a supernatural and peculiar religion to being a religion of moralism and optimism.

In the latter stages—that is, in our own times—human rights have replaced God-given privilege, and the fragmented culture of victimization has replaced the law of love. Although we have traced some of the reasons for this drift, ultimately, of course, unbelief is mysterious. Why does theology lose its vital connection with its source? A full answer to the question is impossible. But it surely happened.

For all its impact, the movement known as Neo-orthodoxy, with Karl Barth as its prime mover, was not able to reverse the trend toward the secularization of natural law. Its tactic was quite the opposite of the "spring" theory. Yet in the name of the radical sovereignty of God, it denied any place at all to general revelation and in fact did much to take natural theology out of circulation altogether.

WHAT SCRIPTURE SAYS

If we are to recover the good part of natural theology and remain faithful to the tradition of Calvin, we must return to Scripture to see what is taught there. The drift toward secularization has been accompanied by an increasingly lifeless reading of Scripture. When theology and preaching become moralistic and rationalistic, their vitality is sapped. Getting back to Scripture has ever been the hallmark of evangelical commitment. Faithfulness to the precept of *semper reformanda* should include the very soul of the theological enterprise. What is even more important than an exhaustive analysis of the secularization of natural law, then, is forging the way to reconstitute natural law in a biblical sense. The great Protestant principle of *sola scriptura* was never so badly needed as today.

In one sense, doing theology should have no trace of originality at all. The most faithful doctrine is simply the correct understanding of the Word of God, applied to various needs. In another way, doing theology is always fresh and vital, first because the Word itself is "living and active, sharper than any two-edged sword" (Heb. 4:12), and second and more fundamentally, because God himself is alive. Our dependence on him is never static.

Insights of Biblical Theology

One of the most promising trends within Protestantism is the Biblical Theology movement,[8] which is now one hundred years old. In 1894 Geerhardus Vos became the first to hold the newly formed chair of biblical theology at Princeton Theological Seminary. His stress throughout his years as a scholar was on biblical exegesis based on awareness of the redemptive-historical character of revelation. Vos taught that biblical theology recognizes revelation as divine activity, and as such reproduces the features of this activity. It especially takes into account the progressive and organic nature of redemption.[9] Vos's legacy includes the work of Herman Ridderbos, Klaas Schilder, S. G. De Graaf, and Richard B. Gaffin.

One of the main consequences of a biblical-theological sensitivity to Scripture is to regard redemptive history as grounded in God's plan, first revealed in the creation. Salvation does not occur in a vacuum: it takes up where creation was interrupted by the Fall. As believers in a fallen world, we marry, we work, we worship God, just as it was commanded at the dawn of history (Gen. 1:28-31). The grace of God in redemption certainly looks forward to full consummation in the new heavens and the new earth. But it also looks back to the original intentions of creation.

Now, it is important for natural law thinking to avoid three pitfalls. The first is to ignore the foundational character of the divine command, based as it is on the state of affairs at creation. The second is to ignore the Fall's severe tempering of the way we perceive that command. Presumably such minimizing is one of the principal ingredients in the secularization of natural law. But the third pitfall is to ignore the way in which redemption in Christ redirects all things toward the heavenly Jerusalem. One of the struggles in the seventeenth century's march toward secular human rights was to show how the Christian way to salvation could have universal appeal. To do this, many apologists limited their focus to the way God reveals himself in creation rather than exploring the cosmic dimension of Christ's redemption. Embarrassed by the particularity of the Gospel, they drew attention to the beauty of creation. Minimizing both sin and the need for redemption, they ended up with a mechanistic universe and a lowest-common-denominator ethics.

A further insight of biblical theology is to notice that the present age, the age of the Gospel, is two-tiered. On the one hand the Church has come into its own and possesses all the benefits of Christ's finished work. We already have every spiritual blessing in the heavenly realms (Eph. 1:3), and all things are ours (I Cor. 3:21-23). On the other hand, we are not yet living in consummate bliss. Sin besets us, and we groan, together with the rest of the creation, longing for full adoption and the full redemption of our bodies (Rom. 8:23).

Already-Not-Yet

The well-known slogan capturing this paradox, first coined by Vos, is *already-not-yet*. Believers live as those who already have full ownership of the world, yet at the same time must learn to wait patiently until that is revealed. The world is the Lord's, and we are his people; yet we live as aliens and pilgrims in that world.

This pause, this hiatus, one in which we have Christ while yet we wait for the Lord (I Thess. 1:9-10), is the context for doing theology. Knowing how to discern God's will by properly interpreting his Word begins with knowing the times in which we live. The Apostle Paul tells his readers in Rome that their ethics must be lived out in an eschatological age: "And do this, understanding the present time. The hour has come for you to wake up from your slumber, because our salvation is nearer now than when we first believed. The night is nearly over; the day is almost here" (Rom. 13:11-12). This passage is all the more significant in that it comes in the practical section of Romans. Beginning with the twelfth chapter, Paul spells out the consequences of the great principles he has enumerated. At the heart of the life of the believer is worshipping God with body and mind (12:1). This means refusing conformity to the world, but renewing the mind in conformity to God's will, and confirming the validity of that will in practice (12:2).

Throughout the final chapters of Romans we feel the paradox of the already–not yet. Because we already live in heaven, we must concentrate on the life of the body of Christ, using our gifts for the benefit of our brothers and sisters (12:6) and being careful to preserve the conscience of weaker believers (14:1–15:4). But because we are not yet in heaven, we need a proper ethic for pilgrims. We must be peacemakers in the world (12:18), going so far as to love our enemies (12:17). We should regard governing authorities as God's ministers and recognize their concern to promote good in society as well as to foster justice (13:1-7). Furthermore, we should have great missionary zeal. The fifteenth chapter of Romans is a paean to world evangelization, using the theme of Christ as choir director of the new song in God's praise (15:7-22). Echoing Jeremiah's famous Letter to the Exiles, Paul enjoins believers, as it were, to "seek the peace and prosperity of the city" (Jer. 29:7).

This teaching is consistent with Paul's other writings, indeed with the entire New Testament. While we invest in this world, we do it only tentatively, holding the things of the world with a light hand. When Paul discusses vocation with the Corinthians, he tells them they may keep their station (I Cor. 7:17, 20). But it is not conservatism to play down the benefits of change. Rather, it is the already-not-yet. If you were called as a slave, seek your freedom, but don't worry if it doesn't come right away (7:21). If you are not married, you may look for a spouse, but it is better to stay single if you are able, because married life adds a burden to the difficulty of worshipping God in a foreign land (25-28). The sum of the matter is that "the time is short." Because of this, if you buy and use the world's goods, don't make strong commitments to them (29-31).

The implications of this already-not-yet theology for natural law are clear. There can be no timeless principles derived from creation alone. Any proper ethic must be cognizant both of the limiting effects of sin and of the temporary nature of the present regime. Although natural law has its place, it is not the Gospel. Furthermore, properly understood it refuses to engage in culture Christianity or to forge social programs that confuse amelioration with salvation. We need to avoid social Pelagianism. Yet, finally, a proper view of natural law should lead us unashamedly to proclaim Christ as the way of salvation for the nations. It should point the world to the only hope of the world, Jesus Christ. Living for the purpose of Christ is not a barrier to the world but its opportunity for liberating ethics.

NATURAL LAW AND PUBLIC DISCOURSE

How can we who believe in one particular truth engage in a credible public discourse with those who do not share our presuppositions? With a renewed vision based on the insights of biblical theology, we can begin to recapture the territory lost because of the secularization of natural law. In particular, if we are faithful to Scripture's threefold motif of creation, fall, and redemption, we can avoid two errors and move ahead along a third way.

The first error is the hope of finding neutral common ground. Christians today are frustrated. In their newfound acceptability in the 1970s, when *Newsweek* magazine designated 1976 the "Year of the Evangelical," they were sure that the road to social transformation through the Gospel was opening before them. But when the eighties passed and the nineties rolled around, with their disappointing yield, power became more and more appealing as a way to effect change. The movement known as theonomy wants to apply the law of God to modern American society in a direct way. The Christian Coalition claims a right to its place at the table of politics. Others are sure that if only people were logical, they could readily believe the compelling logic of the Christian position and embrace it. The difficulty here is not the desire to bring legislation, politics, and human reason into conformity with God's truth, but the way in which that is to be done. We are not yet in the new heaven and new earth. That day will come, but not through programs, or through the ascendancy of biblical law in modern pluralist society.

The other error is to retreat into pietism. This approach holds that if we concentrate on worship and evangelism, social problems will take care of themselves, if they matter at all. There are many variants on this. Surely Karl Barth represents a special version of this view. But so does much of populist evangelicalism. The idea is that the Church is spiritual, and not earthly. Its gaze is heavenward, and its main occupation should be the saving of souls, not social improvement. But being other-worldly is as bad as being coercive. It is true that Christ died on a cross, the ultimate world-denying act. But at the same time he builds his church on the Rock. Christianity is in fact the most world-affirming of all religions.

A Third Way

An approach to natural law is needed that not only avoids these two errors but faithfully reflects the biblical ethic of already-not-yet. Space does not permit a full development of this most important third way; a few suggestions will have to suffice.

First, it is important to recognize what Calvin taught so clearly, that natural law is evident to, and at least to some extent characterizes the awareness of, various peoples. Practically, this means we can assume that everyone knows God and has a moral conscience, at least at some level. Thus if we engage in politics, or law, or any other sphere of public life, we can appeal to what people already know deep down. When we discuss issues with a political opponent, we are facing not a *tabula rasa* but someone who is receiving God's revelation, whether acknowledged or not. Does this mean we must quote Scripture in a debate about abortion or labor laws? Not necessarily. It means we *may* quote Scripture if that helps our argument, but we are not obligated to do so. Since our controlling principle is scripturally derived, every argument that is faithful to biblical principles, whether directly referring to Scripture or not, is sound, and can be persuasive. We do not have to yield to cognitive bargaining to achieve our ends. Nor do we need to be satisfied with lowest-common-denominator ethics, such as virtue or integrity.

Second, we must be realistic about sin and the impediment to natural law brought about by our fallen natures. We are not yet in the new heaven and new earth. Our political action, our artistic pursuits, our parenting should all be done sincerely but without illusions. While we must seek the prosperity and peace of the city, we should place our hope not in it but in the city to come, "whose architect and builder is God" (Heb. 11:12). St. Augustine argued with his Roman critics that placing all hope in the City of God does not make believers less earthly good but, on the contrary, enables them to be more productive in the City of Man.

Third, while we reject relativism, we believe strongly in a differentiated society. Properly applying natural law does not mean a uniform coercion, with a winner-takes-all attitude. It means being clear about the identities of each social institution, from the family to the church, the school, government, the marketplace, and so on. Most of these are not political. Obeying the Christian ethic requires knowing the limits of the church, the state, and the other spheres of society. A bare-bones notion of human rights will not help a great deal here. What is needed is to develop a proper ethic regarding each of the spheres. There are norms for the media, norms for a good marriage, norms for the science laboratory, and so on.

When we have begun to recover these principles, we will then be in continuity with the best of Protestant tradition. We will be able to move from Calvin's balanced theology to the contemporary emphasis on biblical theology, and avoid the secularizing tendency of natural law thinking that is not grounded in Scripture. And we may possibly find a language of public discourse that is compelling.

Comments

Nancy Pearcey: I was interested to find William Edgar quoting from seventeenth-century scientists, like the botanist John Ray and the chemist Robert Boyle. Historically, the moral concept of natural law and the idea of natural law in the physical world were part of the same framework. Creation was seen as a single, coherent order. Certainly one of the causes of modernity was the separation of these two notions of law. Natural law in science was reduced to a mechanistic, autonomous, non-teleological force, and that set moral law adrift from any grounding in an objective order. I don't think we can relegitimize the moral concept of natural law unless we also address the problem of where scientific natural law fits into a Christian framework. We need to restore the concept of lawfulness in the human realm and lawfulness in nature as part of a single order.

William Edgar: The last incarnation of the secularization of natural law is in this terrible separation of *is* and *ought* that Hume announced, and then in Moore's so-called naturalistic fallacy, where if you dare to build rights on anything outside the person you are transgressing some philosophical law. We need to get back to the open universe, where there is more freedom to explore and discover, to see the presence of God, even though there are more threats because it's a less certain universe. I think that's a far better world to be in than one that is closed mechanistically and the moral project is left up for grabs.

James Schall: You all know the passage in Aristotle that says that a little error in the beginning leads to a big error in the end. One of my

---

Note: The participants in this conversation are identified on pages 173-74.

former professors argued that Grotius is really the main turning point, with Machiavelli and Hobbes, to modernity. I have a question for Daniel Westberg: You said in your paper that Grotius "continued to affirm the importance of a theological grounding both for the authority of natural law and for a proper understanding of justice." Did you mean revelational theology, or did you mean a natural theology, as we use the term?

Daniel Westberg: I don't think it's revelation at that point, but I do think that for Grotius it is still important to see the structure of the universe ordered under God. When he says that even if we should concede that there is no God, these principles of social order would still be valid, he's not actually arguing for an autonomous form of natural law.

James Schall: I think that's an intellectual error that had serious consequences later on. If God does not exist, there are no first principles of human nature or human beings. The ultimate consequence is that, yes, we can produce a man who is responsible to nothing other than what we will. That's why I say that the small error in the beginning leads to a great error in the end.

David Coffin: Daniel Westberg said that Grotius might have made this assertion to emphasize the objective character of the moral law. If you were talking to someone who didn't believe in God, and you were trying to assert that a table had certain characteristics, couldn't you imagine saying with respect to the created order: Look, whether there's a God or not, if you make a table with three legs, it's going to fall over; the world operates in such a way that tables with only three legs fall over. This seems to me to be a plausible way of accounting for that remark by Grotius without saying that he's giving up the whole thing. I don't have to do natural theology to prove that tables with three legs fall over. In the same way, you might think that you don't have to refer to the fact that the moral law is grounded in a creator in order to have a person see that law at work in the world.

James Schall: On my uncle's dairy farm, when you milked the cows on a three-legged stool it didn't fall over!

John West: I think we've reached a point in our discussion where some people are promoting what might be called "God talk" and others are promoting what we might call "natural law talk." There seems to be a difference of opinion about which is best in public discourse. Some of the Catholics, whose church has a much greater tradition of reason, are the ones arguing for God-talk, and some of the Protestants, where we may have some problems with the use of reason, at least in recent years, are arguing for natural-law-talk. What it comes down to is that at the core of Western civilization are these two almost irreducible principles: divine revelation and reason. They don't cancel each other out, and in some sense the tension between them is one of the great things about Western civilization. The American Founders, and many people quite a few decades after them, were able to hold these both at the same time. When they cite an authority for something, they appeal to both. I guess that's what I would argue for—to have both God-talk and natural-law-talk.

Russell Hittinger: How can natural-law-talk *be* that without God-talk? You're begging the question. How do you even use the term "law" in connection with it without assuming a theology?

John West: You can't have Thomistic natural law. I would prefer to use the term "natural justice," or even "natural right," some sort of understanding of an objective basis of the moral order, particularly useful for politics and civil discourse.

I would argue that Calvin and even Aquinas, in the older version of natural law, had a very clear role for prudence and equity, and that their view of natural law hearkened back to the ancients rather than being a legal scheme with no exceptions, like an administrative code. You start off with a natural sense of equity, and by the time you get to Grotius or Pufendorf you end up with the California constitution, an administrative code. That's ridiculous; it claims more than can be claimed for natural law, or natural right, or natural justice.

On this idea of common ground: we've heard a lot of comments to the effect that, well, 1996 isn't 1896 or 1796, we don't have these common assumptions anymore. How can we make some of these moral arguments without common assumptions about God and man and the world? When I talk with undergraduates, at secular colleges as well as religious ones, I find that there still is such a thing as common sense. It can be beaten out of you in four years of college; I've seen that happen, where students end up in complete relativism. But with most people you can make arguments about moral principles. It's not a stretch to persuade a person that, for instance, if you make a commitment to someone else, you should keep it even if it hurts you; that's an honorable thing to do. Of course, people may also have an incompatible belief that they hold simultaneously; we Americans are great for holding mutually incompatible beliefs. But in general there is still a common ground you can appeal to.

Daniel Westberg: Several people have mentioned their problems with the term "natural law," and I agree. "Objective moral order" might be better. When people realize the consequences of *not* having an objective order, so that you're responsible for manufacturing your own, it may be easier to talk to them about a moral order that can be theologically described as well.

Michael Uhlmann: The problem with natural law in our time is that nobody agrees on what nature is anymore. If we're going to wrestle with natural law, we have to confront head-on the founders of modernity, specifically Bacon and Hobbes, and ultimately Locke. Taking them on means, in turn, that we have to confute the foundations of non-teleological science, which is a daunting task indeed. Far from seeing nature as a guide, Bacon says you can torture nature for the relief of man's estate. Whatever we may think about that, it works; it produces penicillin. Just as no one in this room, I suspect, would wish to live in Calvin's Geneva, so no one would wish to live without penicillin. But can you have penicillin without Locke?

Another point: Post-Westphalia, there's the whole question of the relation between religion and politics. Founding documents like the Mayflower Compact, which begins, "In the name of God, amen," presuppose a religious people and certify a celestial connection to human affairs. But there are no founding documents of that sort to be seen today. Modern political society is founded on explicitly secular grounds. There is one noble and conspicuous exception: the preamble to the Declaration of Independence, which talks of "self-evident" truths and explicitly acknowledges nature and nature's God as the source of our rights. It's easy to dismiss that sort of talk as so much soft-headed deism, but I submit to you that the preamble to the Declaration is, warts and all, as good as you're going to get in the modern world. It may not be fully up to the standards that those of us in this room would prefer, but if it's too easily dismissed, you don't have anything left; you're naked when the wind blows.

We haven't said much, during our discussions, about the American regime, which is a shame, because it is the regime most closely associated with the law of nature. It also happens to be the regime of which most of us are citizens, and of whose bounty, physical and metaphysical, we take abundant advantage without so much as a bow in its direction. The American regime isn't pure deistic Locke; it combines significant elements of the religious tradition and the Enlightenment. The problem is that the Enlightenment boys have been writing the history books, and the religious tradition is simply written out. But this combination of traditions is what gives the American regime a certain noble possibility, and in our understandable pessimism about the desiccation of modernity we are sometimes inclined to forget that. Where else in what used to be called Christendom could you have, and do you have, conversations like this one? Where else could you have a sizable percentage of the body politic earnestly and honestly engaging issues of morality in the public arena? Nowhere else do you find this, and that's not accidental. I think we too easily dismiss this regime for its shortcomings without paying sufficient attention to its noble qualities and how they could be made stronger.

Keith Pavlischek: How can you know intellectually that the notion of "self-evident" rights is part of the emasculation of the older natural law tradition, that there is nothing self-evident about these propositions, and yet embrace them with a pious reverence?

David Coffin: Is it the case that a theory of natural law is for the sake of the unbeliever but that he has to be persuaded of the theory before it's of any use? It sounds sometimes as if that's what's being suggested: until we get everybody on board the theory, it's not of any help. That seems to me to be singularly wrongheaded. It's as if we had to get some theory of epistemology straightened out before anybody could *know* anything. It seems to me that it's the other way around—we know things, and then we would like to give an account of *how* we know.

Whether anybody agrees on what nature is or not seems to me to be a matter of some indifference to the Christian who wants to try to influence people in the world. Believing that there is a nature, that there is a God, that there is a common morality, he can hope that his efforts will find some point of resonance in the other person, because that person's own theories about himself and the world don't overcome the God-created nature he carries around with him. It seems to me that in that sense natural law is more helpful to inform the believer about what he might anticipate in making arguments grounded in nature, whether the other person acknowledges it or not, because the nature comes through.

One of my teachers, Francis Schaeffer, used to say that when the chairs have been arranged in the chapel, although your presuppositions about where the chairs are may determine how you act, nevertheless, if the chairs really are contrary to your presuppositions in the area where you're walking, you're going to bang your shins. You'll soon get tired of banging your shins and begin to adjust your behavior to avoid the bruises. That way of thinking is helpful. We can know that unbelievers are going to get a lot of bruises, regardless of whether they acknowledge God or a moral order, and we can keep appealing to that and anticipate that, at least for the sake of avoiding the bruises, they might comply.

William Edgar said in his paper that there is a certain kind of mystery attached to unbelief. If we are looking for a system of dealing with public policy or politics that will provide for human flourishing in this world in a wholly certain, virtually mechanical way, we are doomed to failure. There isn't any such system. The human flourishing of societies is dependent upon the good will of God. Unless he blesses those efforts, even the best efforts and arguments will be futile, because of the sinful disposition of man. So the Apostle Paul tells Timothy, "The Lord's bondservant must be gentle, able to teach and to correct those who are erring . . ."—then in the King James it's wonderfully put, "*peradventure God may grant him repentance and a knowledge of the truth.*"

What we can say, then, is this: Natural law tells us that there is a God-created nature and a world. That nature normally flourishes in this world if we live in accordance with God's law. Although sin has radically undermined our ability to do that in any way that is saving to us or honoring to God, sin doesn't prevent us from flourishing in a this-worldly sense by living according to God's law. But unless God himself restrains our sinfulness, it's going to become greater and greater. One of the ways that God restrains it is through this intrinsic sensibility by which we grasp through the mind the moral principles in the world. Another way is through the preaching of the Gospel and the conversion of his creatures and through the witness of the Church.

So in arguments of this kind where unbelievers say, "You have *only* Scripture," the Church can say, "Ha! You have only reason. We have the authority of God himself. Although you foolishly won't listen to this, it informs our life. You are in danger of the judgment of God if you fail to listen to this authority." That also works on the conscience and makes the natural law argument more effective, because they begin to worry, "Suppose my reasoning on this isn't so hot and there actually is a Lord God of Heaven and Earth who thunders from Sinai and delivers the law and I'm going to face him." The correspondence of those two things in a culture, then, makes possible, with the blessing of God, the kind of civilization we've enjoyed. But still it's only *peradventure*. That, I think, is what it means to be creatures.

Paul Marshall: God made it into the Canadian constitution in 1981 because the government engaged in its usual means of public analysis: it did a public opinion poll and 93 per cent of the population wanted God in their constitution. I want to affirm that arguments from the Bible are perfectly legitimate arguments within the American polity. They make more sense to most of the population than other forms of argument. A public space should be open to all the people within the country to offer their arguments.

Michael Cromartie: It was clear that Clarence Thomas not only couldn't make biblical arguments but couldn't even make natural law arguments during his confirmation hearing in Congress.

Russell Hittinger: Senator Biden could.

Michael Uhlmann: Robert Bork was bashed by Senator Biden (a Catholic, by the way) because he didn't embrace natural law. This was the same Joe Biden who bashed Clarence Thomas for *invoking* natural law.

David Smolin: But Thomas invoked the wrong kind of natural law. It was the kind that limits and says no. The good kind gives you all these rights to do whatever you want to do. That's the kind Senator Biden approves of.

Paul Marshall: We must not give the impression that we accept the assertion that these are in principle the legitimate boundaries of public debate. The fact that Clarence Thomas had those problems is of course itself a problem. But these forms of discourse are perfectly decent arguments, and we should defend our right to use them. We need to resist the attempts to say that only certain forms of liberal discourse are appropriate for public discussion in the United States.

Russell Hittinger: It's as if these guys were saying, "Here are my premises; trick me out of them. If you can, you have a successful natural law argument." Unfortunately, this is taken to be the example of what natural law arguments are all about.

Keith Pavlischek: To follow up on what Paul Marshall was saying about surrendering the terms of the debate: In the recent philosophical movement that has been coined Reformed epistemology, philosophers like Alvin Plantiga and Nicholas Wolterstorff are boldly saying to their critics: "I am within my epistemic rights to proceed in building my worldview on the assumption that God exists. It's your burden to prove that I am not within my rights in believing that God exists, and that in building my view of things on that assumption I am irrational." That changes the terms of the debate. Why should the burden be on me to prove that God exists or that there is a binding moral order?

David Coffin: I have the greatest respect for what those Christian philosophers are doing, but that is distinctly different from what is going on here. They're saying that I don't have to do Christian philosophy on the terms set by non-Christians. Of course not. But here we're talking about a common life, not about Christian enclaves where we can do our Christian society and other folk can do other kinds of societies. We're talking about a society where there are Christians and non-Christians, and asking with what means, if any, we can find grounds for some commonality.

Keith Pavlischek: But why can't I take the truths I know from revelation as well as the truths I gain through experience as a basis for my reflection on things like marriage law?

David Coffin: No reason.

Keith Pavlischek: Then those truths ought to be considered publicly accessible as well. That's my point.

David Coffin: I have no objection to that *per se,* but when you talk about "publicly accessible," do you mean accessible to those who deny that Christianity is a revelation from God? If you want to appeal to them, you've got to find something that *is* accessible to them.

Paul Marshall: I'm not quite sure what "publicly accessible" means. Liberal arguments are not "accessible" to many Christians and to others. My point is simply that the public is a space, and you'd better not put boundaries on it.

David Coffin: Do I have any hope of voluntary compliance from a totally depraved person with respect to the truth of God in the public order? Yes, I do. I have that hope because of the way God has created the world and that person. If he won't listen to the authority of God declared in Scripture, I have the hope that there might be other reasons for him to comply voluntarily with this moral order, even though he objects to the idea that God created it.

Keith Pavlischek: I don't disagree with that; I'm just not sure that what counts as publicly accessible has to be that low-flying.

David Coffin: It's entirely individual. There's no standard of public accessibility: it's per person.

Keith Pavlischek: But what counts as publically accessible is going to depend on the degree of public consensus. If we increasingly disagree about basic moral truths, then what counts as publicly accessible gets smaller and smaller.

Joan O'Donovan: I'm trying to recall—no doubt I'll do it badly—what Karl Barth replied to someone who said to him, "You know, Professor Barth, that you've got to put yourself in the other person's place and talk to people where they are." That has become a slogan for how apologetics should be done in the public forum. To which Karl Barth said, "Well, I am. I'm putting myself at the foot of the cross, and that is where they are." That's where reason finds its jumping-off point. The hope, in that situation, is no more or no less than the hope for revelation in Jesus Christ. Every single person whom we meet is at the foot of the cross, and that is where we address everyone.

Carl Henry: I wonder whether we have elevated to priority a program relevant specially to the elite, who probably offer the least reason for expecting that they would hear it under any circumstances. I've been trolling with you on the bottom of the ocean for two days, and I'm still not sure what I'm trolling for. Are we wholly persuaded that if we could properly define natural law and raise this banner, it would save Western culture from the graveyard? Are we fighting fire with half of the water supply? I presume that we all agree, within our different traditions, that salvation is in Christ and in Christ alone. I realize we're meeting here for a specific purpose, not to discuss the whole agenda. But I know that when the Roman Empire fell, the nobility didn't rally the troops to forge a more articulate doctrine of natural law. They went about their business, confident that everything was all right, and it was really the slaves whom the nobles despised who carried the moral order into the future.

David Coffin: I confess that part of my interest in natural law is not only as a way of approaching unbelievers but to protect me from believers today. It seems to me that there is a serious threat from Christians who, not confident that there is some way of addressing an unbelieving world, seem to be seriously contemplating the only other options, evangelism and conquest. I find the latter quite a terrifying specter.

Carl Henry: It is as important for the representation of God to say that God wills justice as it is to say that God wills that you be born again. The Gospel, properly understood, includes both dimensions, and the two must be held together.

William Edgar: As Dr. Henry said, after Rome fell it was slaves and other people in various echelons of society who were used to re-salt and re-light the world and bring a wonderful civilization to replace decadent Rome. Surely one of the things that God also does in situations like that is raise up leaders, articulate leaders who can respond to those who charge them wrongly and also encourage the Church to have a proper response itself. Obviously one of the greatest leaders of all time was Augustine, who responded in a masterpiece of theological writing and apologetics to what was basically a charge coming at the end of a long tradition of pagan charges against Christians. That charge said, Why was Rome sacked by Alaric? It was because of the Church, because of Christians. The gods who had pledged themselves to protect Rome wouldn't do it anymore because there was this intrusive God who claimed to be the creator and wouldn't play ball with the others. That was disturbing the unity, so the gods now refused to protect the city.

We have something like that today. People who believe in truth are charged with being the reason why others don't get along, and why society doesn't work. Augustine answered in this masterpiece where he said: There are two cities, the City of God and the City of Man. The City of God is certainly what we are hoping for; it's God himself in his kingdom. But far from being so heavenly-minded that they are of no earthly good, Christians are among the best citizens. They have the most cogent social programs; their work with the poor is exemplary. Augustine makes suggestions along that line, suggestions for politics. While *The City of God* is a treatise against paganism in some respects, it's also about social action for Christians. This I think is faithful, ultimately, to Paul's argument in Romans 12. The way to change society is to worship, and then, yes, be kind to the weaker brother, yes, begin to pray for your politicians, and go into politics too. If you're in politics, be a good politician, do your job well. But never lose sight of your ultimate goal. To me that goes a long way towards solving the problem and giving the opportunity for natural law.

4

The Concept of Rights in Christian Moral Discourse

Joan Lockwood O'Donovan

For both Christian and non-Christian political and social thinkers, the language of fundamental human rights is the modern substitute for the older theological language of natural law. The entrenchment of rights language in contemporary political and legal discourse is beyond dispute. Less obvious, but no less significant, are indications that the concept of rights is itself passing beyond dispute, and possibly even beyond discussion. One such indication is the frustrating absence from Oxford libraries and bookshops of most of the philosophical and virtually all of the theological treatments of rights published between 1950 and 1985 (papal encyclicals excluded), as contrasted with the omnipresence of publications on human rights law and its enforcement.[1]

One possible explanation is that the considerable American and European interest over this period in the philosophy and theology of rights has attracted only minor academic attention in England (at least in Oxford), despite the ongoing and expanding jurisprudential concern with rights fostered by international and European Community

Joan Lockwood O'Donovan lectures, tutors, and writes in Oxford, England. She is the author of *Theology of Law and Authority in the English Reformation* and of *George Grant and the Twilight of Justice* and is co-editing a sourcebook of readings in the history of Christian political thought.

law. Were this the case, the most plausible reason would be the greater hold of the liberal *utilitarian* tradition on post-war English moral and political thought as compared with the greater hold of the liberal *contractarian* tradition on American and European moral and political thought.

As this conjecture implies, the concept of subjective rights, or rights ascribable to individuals and groups, has entered contemporary political and legal currency primarily through the liberal contractarian tradition bequeathed by Hobbes and Locke, Rousseau and Kant, and the theoretical exponents of the American and French Revolutions (though admittedly this tradition has incorporated a good deal of utilitarian logic). Consequently, the meanings of the term "rights" in both popular and scholarly usage cannot be properly ascertained in detachment from this theoretical context that has been formative for political, moral, and theological orientations in this century. For these meanings are embedded in a constellation of political-legal, philosophical, and theological concepts with a complex history: concepts of divine, natural, and positive law, of justice, freedom, and equality, of reason and will, of sovereignty and property, of covenant and contract.

My impression is that theologians often engage in a naïve and facile appropriation of the language of rights. Across denominational boundaries there is a quite predictable argument, running from the creation of humankind in God's image to the unique dignity of persons in community to their universal possession of rights. Different denominations do bring important nuances to the argument: Reformed theologians emphasize human partnership in God's covenant and lordship over creation, Lutherans emphasize Christ's universal justification of humanity on the cross, and Catholics emphasize the renovation of the divine image by the incarnate grace of Christ. Nevertheless, there appears to be a consensus about the unproblematic nature of the move from human dignity to human rights once the theological "foundation" or "analogy" is prepared. "Rights" is accepted by all as adequately expressing the moral attributes of a theologically conceived humanity.[2] However, it is precisely the adequacy of "rights" as an element of theological-moral discourse that I wish to challenge, in the light of the pre-modern traditions of Christian natural law, particularly the Augustinian tradition with its evangelical and Christological approach to natural law.

Two Orientations Toward Political Right

A close analysis of the history of the concept of subjective rights in the light of earlier theological-political conceptualization reveals a progressive antagonism between the older Christian tradition of politi cal right and the newer voluntarist, individualist, and subjectivist orientation. The contrasting logic of the two orientations may be conveyed quite simply: whereas in the older patristic and medieval tradition, God's right established a matrix of divine, natural, and human laws or objective obligations that constituted the ordering justice of political community, in the newer tradition God's right established discrete rights, possessed by individuals originally and by communities derivatively, that determined civil order and justice.

In the older traditions, the central moral-political act on the part of ruler and ruled alike was to consent to the demands of justice, to the obligations inhering in communal life according to divine intention and rationally conceived as laws. The ruler commanded, legislated, and issued binding judgments, but these acts were to embody his consent to an order of right and obligation binding his own will. The subject was obligated to obey the ruler's commands, statutes, and judgments, not only because of his rightful authority, but also because these acts conformed to the requirements of justice.

In the newer orientation to political right that began to emerge in the fourteenth and fifteenth centuries, the active individual will occupied a central position. Its seminal moral-political acts were conceived as modes of subjecting its social environment. So, on the one hand, the Roman civil lawyers stressed the source of positive law in the commanding will of the ruler, and on the other hand, certain theologians attributed to individuals pre-political "natural" rights or powers that placed moral-legal constraints on the operation of political authority, sometimes by way of the mechanism of a social or political contract.[3] It is important to note, however, that both lawyers and theologians regarded the original rights belonging—by divine ordination—to natural political societies as corporate persons (whether or not formed by compact) to be more determinative of civil organization and legislation than the original rights of individuals.

Not until the seventeenth and eighteenth centuries did the subjective rights of individuals supercede the objective right of divinely revealed and natural laws as the primary or exclusive basis of political authority, justice, and law. These centuries dominated the transformation of the Western Christian tradition of natural law and natural right into a tradition of natural *rights*.

The theoretical elaborations of the concept of rights from the fifteenth to the eighteenth centuries, but especially in its classical and Enlightenment heydays, have invested it with lasting intellectual content. For contemporary moral and political theorizing this content is in varying degrees inescapable, being woven into the fabric of politics in this century—the fabric of democratic, pluralistic, technological liberalism. Christian political thought (both Catholic and Protestant) that is not wholly satisfied with this fabric recognizes the need to divest the concept of rights of its offensive theoretical material. But when it attempts to separate some conceptual threads from the fabric, the result inevitably falls short: either too much of the fabric adheres to the threads, or the threads lose their coherence.

To substantiate this judgment by reviewing the range of contemporary theological treatments of human rights would require prior completion of two formidable intellectual tasks: first, to delineate the inherited theoretical content of the Western "rights" tradition, and second, to demonstrate the incompatibility of this content with the biblical theological doctrines that Christians regularly (and necessarily) invoke to ground the concept of rights. I propose to undertake the first of these prior tasks, with the hope of helping readers judge for themselves the historical and theological plausibility of contemporary Christian appropriations of the language of rights. I will consider the central historical content of rights theories that is theologically problematic in three categories: the roles played by property rights, contract, and freedom of choice.

THE ROLE OF PROPERTY RIGHTS

Property rights occupied a paradigmatic position in early, influential definitions of subjective rights, and have decisively shaped subsequent theoretical developments. A late medieval milestone was Pope John XXII's attack in the 1320s on the Franciscan Order's vow of absolute poverty, which entailed the individual and communal renunciation of all legal rights of ownership of the material goods used by members of the order. Against the vow, the pope contended that all lawful consumption of material goods was inseparable from property right in them or dominion *(dominium)* over them.[4] He reinforced his case with the important assertion that *dominium,* in the legal sense of full property right over earthly goods, belonged to Adam in his created state and reflected the divine *dominium* over the earth.[5] In arguing thus (against the Augustinian mainstream)[6] the pope anchored property right in an original created human power of disposal or control over temporal things. His opponent, the nominalist William of Ockham, while defending a non-proprietary, natural (as opposed to legal) "right of use" of external objects, nevertheless defined individual right as a subjective "power."[7]

In the fourteenth and fifteenth centuries, the idea of right *(ius)* as a power belonging to a subject was carried forward by the Parisian nominalist Jean Gerson (1363-1429) and his followers.[8] Gerson extensively explicated the concept of *ius* as "a dispositional *facultas* or power, appropriate to someone and in accordance with the dictates of right reason," and he conceived "natural *dominium*" as the divinely bestowed *ius* of "every creature" to "take inferior things into its own use for its own preservation." Furthermore, Gerson joined to man's "natural *dominium*" the *dominium* or *facultas* of liberty.[9] He thus paralleled man's original property right—his power of using exterior things —with his original freedom—his power of using himself, his body, and his actions.

It remained for political and legal philosophers in the sixteenth and seventeenth centuries to draw radical conclusions from Gerson's assimilation of human freedom to property right. Under Gersonian influence, two powerful theorists of the Salamanca school in Spain, the Jesuits Luis de Molina and Francisco Suárez, concluded that men, having by nature an active *facultas* or *dominium* in their liberty, could lawfully alienate it and enslave themselves.[10] According to Suárez, not only private individuals but political communities could lawfully contract away their freedom and other property, and both were obliged by the law of nature to honor the terms of their agreement, no matter how detrimental to their own welfare.[11] In addition, both Suárez and Molina universalized the Gersonian concept of *iura* as moral *facultates* possessed by subjects to include the passive entitlements of subjects to things not yet possessed *(ius ad rem)*, such as the right of the laborer to his wages.[12] The meaning of this move was subsequently revealed by the Dutch jurist Hugo Grotius, in his definition of such a claim-right as "the faculty of demanding what is due . . . [to which] answers the obligation of rendering what is owing. . . ."[13]

Hobbes, Locke, and the Levellers

The seventeenth-century proprietary concept of subjective right arrived at its zenith with the political writings of Hobbes and Locke and the Leveller manifestoes. Its essence, containing the seeds of future developments, was an understanding of the individual as "free inasmuch as he is the proprietor of his person and capacities," his freedom being conceived as both independence of "the wills of others" and "a function of possession."[14] Hobbes's chief contribution to this vision was his conception of "right of nature" as the individual's unrestrained liberty "to use his own power" and to act for his self-preservation.[15] Against the earlier Scholastic and Gersonian rights theory, Hobbes's conception asserted the radical priority of natural right to natural law and the radical separation of natural right from social obligation. In their natural condition, Hobbes's individuals have an unlimited right to use everything, including one another's bodies, unbounded by obligations of natural justice.[16] Only the intolerable insecurity of right in this condition necessitates the prudential stratagems tor peace known as "laws of nature," which include the "mutual [contractual] transferring of right" by individuals to a civil power recognized by them for the purpose of securing to them a sphere of limited rights.[17] The one portion of individual right that is, however, inalienable is the right to one's life and to the means of defending it, and the citizen may by right forcibly resist violent assaults on these fundamental possessions by the civil power itself.[18]

If Hobbes's emphasis on the unlimited content of natural right gave rise to a model of social relationships as generally acquisitive, atomistic, and competitive, the Levellers' and Locke's concentration on property right gave rise to a proto-liberal economic or market model of social relationships. As the following excerpt from a tract of Richard Overton demonstrates, the Levellers foreshadowed the American Revolutionary writers in their complete assimilation of subjective right to property:

To every Individuall in nature is given an individual property by nature, not to be invaded or usurped by any: for every one as he is himselfe, so he hath a selfe propriety, else could he not be himselfe, and on this no second may presume to deprive any of, without manifest violation and affront to the very principles of nature, and of the Rules of equity and Justice between man and man; mine and thine cannot be, except this be; No man hath power over my rights and liberties, and I over no mans; . . . and as we are delivered of God by the hand of nature into this world, every one with a natural, innate freedome and propriety . . . even so are we to live, every one equally and alike to enjoy his Birth-right and privilege; even all whereof God by nature hath made him free.[19]

Not only does Overton conceive the individual's property in himself as an exclusive power of disposal effective against the whole world (the classical Roman-law sense of *dominium*), but, as C. B. Macpherson astutely observes, he identifies his total self-possession, his "'freedom from other men,'" with his essential humanity. Macpherson shows how "this concept of man's essence as freedom, and freedom as the active proprietorship of one's person and capacities," underpinned all the Levellers' claims for specific "civil, religious, economic, and political" rights:

As to civil and religious liberty, it was plain, first, that property in one's own person required a guaranteed freedom from arbitrary arrest, trial, and imprisonment, and the right to due process of law. It was equally plain that property in one's own mental and spiritual person required freedom of speech, publication, and religion. . . . The basic economic right was of course the right to individual property in goods and estate, which included the right not only to own but to acquire by the free exercise of a man's own energies and capacities. The particular economic rights the Levellers demanded—freedom to buy, sell, produce, and trade, without licence, monopoly, arbitrary regulation, or arbitrary taxation—were evident corollaries.[20]

Significantly, the Levellers' proprietary underpinning of subjective rights caused them to refuse the extension of the electoral franchise to classes of persons such as servants and alms-takers who had alienated or forfeited "active proprietorship" of their natural capacity for work.[21]

The principal advance of Locke beyond the Levellers was his elaboration of certain internal relationships among subjective rights as forms of property. The most important of these was the relationship between the individual's ownership of his capacity to labor and his ownership of the produce of his labor. On analogy with God's exclusive proprietary right over his creation, Locke's individual has exclusive proprietary right over the objects created by his work (i.e., his action on his material environment) within the broad rational constraints of natural law. The individual's control of his labor is merely one aspect of his autonomous freedom—his right of unrestrained disposal of his actions apart from the obligations belonging to the natural law: hence, his acquisition of material property presumes a sphere of moral autonomy.[22]

Exchanging Natural Right for Civil Right

The centrality of property in labor for Locke's theory of private property focused attention on the consequences of alienating one's labor by a wage contract, and so on the quality of labor as a transferable commodity. These considerations threw into sharp relief the question of what portion of natural right was alienable (whether by political or economic transaction) and what was inalienable. A century later this question would occupy the forefront of American Revolutionary thought, and the answer proposed by Thomas Paine revealed the outer limit of libertarian individualism. According to Paine, each individual upon entering into society retains those natural rights "in which the power to execute is as perfect in the individual as the right itself" (e.g., "rights of the mind") and "deposits . . . in the common stock of society" those in which, "though the right is perfect in the individual, the power to execute them is defective" (e.g., the individual's "right to judge in his own cause"). In conceiving the exchange of natural right for civil right, Paine draws on the analogy of a joint stock company: "Every man is proprietor in society, and draws on the capital as a matter of right."[23]

The continuing predominance of property right within the negative libertarian tradition is hardly surprising. It sustains the concept of a right or freedom as a power of acting possessed by a subject that entails the obligation of non-interference on the part of all other subjects, and especially of government.[24] The influence of property right on the more recent tradition of positive or welfare rights is less obvious. For welfare rights are "entitlements" of subjects to goods or opportunities that others alone or in part can provide—e.g., medical care, education, housing, pension security, employment, voting opportunity. If such entitlements signify no more than the moral and/or legal obligations that certain others are under to provide these benefits, then they do not in any sense express property right. But if they constitute obligation-imposing demands on others made by subjects on the basis of their powers of action, then they remain within the ambit of property rights.

The strongest evidence for the latter interpretation is the historical sequence of rights theory, in which negative freedoms have preceded positive welfare claims and so supplied the framework for their conceptualization. The logic of the transition, discernible in much of the contemporary theoretical endorsement of welfare rights and congruent with other manifestations of our subjectivist, voluntarist, and technological culture, is that individuals are impeded in fully using their personal property (their freedoms, powers, or capacities) because the necessary means are unavailable to them. Their property in these capacities implies their claim-right to these means. That claim-right is held against the government, which has, therefore, the duty to provide the relevant means.[25] To understand why the claim-right is held against the government is to understand something of the evolving role of contract in Western political rights theory.

THE ROLE OF CONTRACT

In all Western theories of individual natural rights, the idea of contract has proved indispensable to the theoretical transition from original right to civil and social rights. Contract has regularly been invoked at two conceptual junctures in this transition: at the formation of political society and at the establishment of government, which frequently form one unified moment in the more radical rights theories. It should be noted that the contract of government,[26] broadly conceived as a moral pact or covenant binding ruler and ruled, is not historically coterminous with the appearance of natural rights theory, but precedes it. Pre-Renaissance political pacts and covenants typically expressed the reciprocity of obligation between the monarch and his subjects rooted in their mutual subordination to divine, natural, and ancient-customary laws. Where "rights" of ruler and ruled were protected by such agreements (actual or hypothetical), these "rights" were freedoms and privileges attaching to diverse statuses within a communal-jurisdictional-proprietary network; the point of the contract was largely to circumscribe the royal authority by lesser or, in the case of the Church, different authorities. The paradigmatic influence of Old Testament covenants on these Christian political pacts ensured that promises of obedience to divine (natural and revealed) laws and purposes would constitute a leading part of their content.[27]

In the sixteenth and seventeenth centuries, both Protestant and Catholic theories of political covenant integrated individualist and naturalist ideas, such as the pre-political natural equality of men, their primitive solitary existence, and the inauguration of society by a deliberate agreement among free individuals.[28] For the most part, however, these ideas were set within a solid matrix of more traditional theo-political premises concerning man's natural sociality, God's ordination and institution of political authority and of rulers, and the formation and regulation of communal relations according to divinely given and rationally apprehended principles of justice and charity. Nevertheless, certain Catholic neo-scholastics, such as the Spanish Jesuits Mariana and Suárez, and Protestant natural law thinkers schooled in German and Dutch federalism, such as Althusius and Grotius, offered strikingly contractualist accounts of political society and (except for Grotius) of government.[29]

The Exchange of Rights

The crucially novel element introduced into social and political contract conceptions by the more radical English Puritans and Whigs from the mid-seventeenth century onward was the idea of an exchange of rights—of natural for civil rights. This idea resonated with commercial overtones. The basis of political society and rule was thereby brought into the sphere of economic transaction. The effect was to accentuate the superior bargaining position and adjudicating power of contracting individuals or associations of individuals and the dominant role of calculative rationality in setting the terms of the contract. Another effect was to deprive the sphere of *public* welfare and public law of a moral basis independent from that of *private* welfare and private law. Although this derivation of public right from private right did not prevent seventeenth-century theorists such as Selden and Hobbes from erecting highly regulative and dictatorial states, the longer-term outcome would be to undermine the independent purposes and operation of the public realm.

As the transcendent guidance of revealed and natural law, recognized by most seventeenth-century rights theories, has gone further into eclipse, it has become clearer that such independence of the public realm requires a basis beyond the mutual limiting of individual wills and a logic beyond prudential strategies for enhancing personal property. In contemporary contractarian liberalism, all communal obligations are derived from contract, and the only residual social right is the creation of free-market forces. It is hardly surprising in this theoretical climate that political authority and action should themselves succumb to the logic and principles of market economics, and not only in academic theory and popular ideology but in the practical details of political life. Contemporary political theorists, enamoured of neo-classical economics, have conceived the state as "a business run by entrepreneurs," political parties as "firms trying to maximize votes," and "voting preferences as utility functions." What is more, politicians, as Ian Shapiro points out, "sell a commodity as entrepreneurs, employ agencies to 'package' their products for advertising, and gear those products to what they believe the market demands."[30]

Correspondingly, citizens in their dealings with the state are increasingly consumer-conscious: they seek the most advantageous political exchange, the best possible protection and provision for their indefinitely expanding range of personal rights in return for surrender of some freedom and material property. On the basis of their ever more explicit contractual relations with the state, as formalized in bills and charters of rights, citizens have growing incentives and opportunities to demand legal redress of the failures of governmental and public agencies to furnish the expected goods and services. Such political contractualism spells the most extreme reduction of public law and the common good it enforces to private law and private good.

FREEDOM OF CHOICE, THE UNIVERSAL RIGHT

In a society whose only coherent public moral language is that of subjective rights, whether of individuals or groups, the only universally respected right is that of freedom, understood as the sovereignty of the subject over his physical and moral world—that is, his emancipation from all externally imposed material and spiritual constraints on his freedom of choice and self-determination. A common thread throughout rights theories from their inception is the idea of the bearer of rights as a self-transcending will who uses the world around as well as his own body and capacities to achieve certain self-referential ends. Even if these ends and the means of realizing them are given in divine and natural law, the rights-bearer is still regarded as the primary source of political meaning, social worth, and positive law; if they are not so given, then the rights-bearer is regarded as the exclusive source. The secularization of liberalism in the eighteenth and nineteenth centuries has meant that the self-positing, personal creative will acknowledges fewer and fewer external obligations and objective goods.

It is precisely on account of the supposed sovereignty of the rights-bearing subject, relative or absolute, that the concept of rights is not simply coordinate with the concept of obligations, as some more conservative apologists for rights wish to argue.[31] As Shapiro's analysis of John Rawls and Robert Nozick amply demonstrates, the "workmanship model" basis for classical rights theories continues to confer "asymmetrical rights on the agent or maker" that impose obligations on others.[32] The resulting situation is a competition among sovereign subjects to maximize their freedom, i.e., to maximize protection of and provision for their rights. General belief in the equality of subjects in respect of rights entails rights-bearers in honoring the claims of others, but only insofar as their legitimate prudential calculations allow. Conflicts among right-claims, therefore, can be resolved only by pragmatic compromises.

Resolving such conflicts within the contractarian tradition has been rendered even more difficult by the absorption of utilitarian interest theory, which presents individual judgments about utility as highly subjective, and as such incommensurable. The outcome of stressing the incommensurability of "interest" or "utility" judgments is to focus public consensus on freedom of choice as the pivotal right.

Concluding Observations

Our task has been to examine historically and critically the three dominant conceptual elements of the Western tradition of rights theory: property right, contract, and freedom of choice. Within this tradition, as we have seen, the rights-bearing subject has been conceived as the exclusive proprietor both of his spiritual and physical being and capacities and of those external objects necessary to their preservation and development. His orientation to his environment has been portrayed as controlling, acquisitive, and competitive: he disposes, uses, exchanges, commands, and demands. His freedom as self-possession consists in independence from, or non-subjection to, other wills, externally imposed obligations, and natural limitations. The self-possessing subject forms social and political relationships through the formal (whether real or hypothetical) mechanism of the contract, whose terms typically mirror those of an economic transaction undertaken from calculations of self-interest.

To anticipate for a moment the theological task that should follow the historical one attempted here: it may appear facile to argue the incompatibility of unadulterated secular liberalism with the Christian doctrines that are regularly invoked to support the generic concept of human rights—those of the *imago Dei,* the divine-human covenant, and sinful humanity's justification and freedom in Christ. At a certain level this incompatibility is obvious to all current Christian apologists for rights, many of whom have explicitly disowned elements of secular liberal theory. But the question that has yet to be satisfactorily answered—one that I hope my historical analysis has sharpened—is why Christian thinkers have been and are willing to adopt a child of such questionable parentage as the concept of human rights.[33]

The answer, I suggest, lies in the affinities between some modern theological interpretations of these biblical doctrines and the classical liberal anthropological premises. The theological exercise I am recommending would at least indirectly clarify these affinities. It would present theological alternatives to, for instance, interpreting the *imago Dei* as human participation in God's rational, self-positing freedom, and interpreting the covenant as human partnership in God's sovereign, creative ordering of the world. Both of these interpretations, combined in the popular concept of "responsibility," are more open to the political-ethical language of subjective rights than to that of objective rights and obligations.

Amidst the universal political enthusiasm for rights in the civilized world, theologians with reservations about the concept are in an unenviable position. In attacking what has become a virtually unassailable datum of the Christian social conscience, we run the risk of being mistaken for complacent pietists or atavistic romantics. At the least we expose ourselves to the accusation of being unconcerned with the apologetic equipment of Christian evangelism.

However, there are enough signs about of social anomie, moral confusion, and ideological fatigue to suggest that the risk is worth taking. We may, after all, be witnessing the bitter historical irony that the revitalized striving in contemporary society for the substance of community, reciprocity, equity, and public trust is being undermined by its most trusted theoretical support.

A Response

Robert P. George

In examining the concept of rights in moral discourse, Joan O'Donovan argues, in effect, that Christians can and should dispense with
the language of rights. Her belief in the incompatibility of "rights-talk"
with authentically Christian moral and political discourse derives from
her judgment that the modern liberal concept of rights belongs to the
socially atomistic and disintegrative philosophy of possessive individualism, in which, she says, "freedom as self-possession consists in
independence from, or non-subjection to, other wills, externally imposed obligations, and natural limitations."

But in precisely what sense does the concept of rights belong to
this admittedly corrupt philosophy? Dr. O'Donovan suggests that it
does so in a historical sense. The concept emerged as part of the
philosophy of liberalism—and, one might add, liberalism can't do
without it. But surely no mere historical connection is sufficient to
establish that those who reject possessive individualism cannot now
deploy the language of rights without thereby importing into their
thought features of that philosophy that mark it as antithetical to the
value of community and other important human goods. Here, I would
suggest, only a logical (or, at a minimum, a very strong psychological)
connection will suffice.

Of course, on one possible interpretation of what Dr. O'Donovan
is claiming, the proposition that the *modern liberal* concept of rights
belongs to the philosophy of possessive individualism states a neces-

---

Robert P. George teaches legal philosophy and civil liberties at Princeton
University and is a practicing constitutional lawyer. He is the author of
Making Men Moral: Civil Liberties and Public Morality, and he currently serves
on the United States Commission on Civil Rights.

sary truth. But this interpretation may, I think, safely be set aside, for it would render the claim singularly uninteresting and, in any event, inadequate to overcome the claims of the neo-Thomists and neo-Calvinists whom she wishes to challenge. The question, remember, is whether the language of rights is unavoidably incompatible with Christian moral discourse. And we are justified in saying yes, I think, only if it can be shown that the modern liberal concept of rights is the only possible concept of rights. This is what neo-Thomists and neo-Calvinists deny. So the burden of Dr. O'Donovan's argument must be to show—against the claims of neo-Thomists and neo-Calvinists—that the concept of rights is in itself a possessive individualist notion.

That, I think, her otherwise wonderfully illuminating historical analysis fails to do. And I strongly suspect that it fails for the simple reason that historical analysis by itself cannot establish the logical (or even the strongly psychological) connection she needs to demonstrate.

Rights-Talk: Useful But Dispensable

My own view is that the language of rights has no intrinsic connection to possessive individualism, though I agree that there is a strong historical connection. This is not to say that I think the language of rights is indispensable. It is not. Rights-claims are claims in justice, and any such claim can be translated out of the language of rights without loss of moral content. The language of rights is, however, useful in the analysis of propositions about justice. It has, as John Finnis has suggested, a suppleness that facilitates the elucidation and evaluation of such propositions.

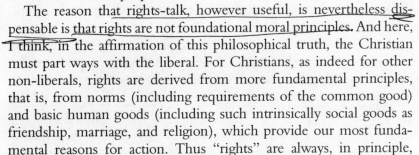

The reason that rights-talk, however useful, is nevertheless dispensable is that rights are not foundational moral principles. And here, I think, in the affirmation of this philosophical truth, the Christian must part ways with the liberal. For Christians, as indeed for other non-liberals, rights are derived from more fundamental principles, that is, from norms (including requirements of the common good) and basic human goods (including such intrinsically social goods as friendship, marriage, and religion), which provide our most fundamental reasons for action. Thus "rights" are always, in principle, reducible to more basic principles. (This is not to suggest that it makes no sense to speak of basic or fundamental human rights.)

Dr. O'Donovan is correct, I think, in identifying liberalism with the voluntarism, positivism, and individualism that emerged in the thinking of influential philosophers and theologians in the fourteenth and fifteenth centuries. I would add that liberalism, as we know it —that is, as it presents itself in advocating rights to abortion, sexual freedom, euthanasia, recreational drug use, and the like—is strongly marked by (1) a dualistic understanding of human beings as conscious and desiring "selves" who inhabit and use subpersonal bodies ("person/body dualism"), and (2) a non-cognitivist understanding of human motivation and practical understanding that reduces reason to, in Hume's evocative phrase, "the slave of the passions." But I would argue that it is these features of liberalism, and not the concept of rights, that are incompatible with Christianity and the Christian (though not only the Christian) understanding of community and its value.

True, the liberal cannot abandon the concept of rights (or "subjective" rights) without ceasing to be a liberal. But the Christian can deploy the concept without compromising his Christianity. By contrast, for a Christian to embrace voluntarism, positivism (in the sense Dr. O'Donovan intends), individualism, person/body dualism, or non-cognitivism is precisely to compromise his Christianity.

But isn't the concept of rights intrinsically selfish? How can it be used by anyone who wishes to follow Christ's injunctions? Well, the concept of justice is not intrinsically selfish. And the concept of rights, as deployed in the work of faithful Christian moral or political thinkers, helps in the analysis of what is just and unjust in the various realms of human intercourse. True, its explanatory standpoint is that of the person whose interests—including an interest in freedom— are at stake in respect of a particular possible decision or action, but I don't see why that is especially problematic from the Christian point of view. Fairness (or unfairness) is always fairness (or unfairness) *to someone*—someone whose interests are at stake. Whether or not we deploy the language of rights, attention to those interests is essential for determining the fairness of any distributional, corrective, or retributive decision.

Rights-Claims: True or False

At the end of the day, rights-claims, to the extent that they are coherent and meaningful, are either true or false. We can, for reasons of prudence, choose to avoid the language of rights—we can, as I say, reduce even true propositions about rights to more fundamental principles—but that will not alter the truth of any true proposition that someone chooses to state in terms of rights. True propositions about rights can be stated, just in case some propositions about justice can be translated into the language of rights. And often enough, such translations really are possible. Take the right to life, or, more precisely, the right of innocent human beings not to be directly killed. This right obtains (i.e., exists as a moral reality) just in case the direct killing of an innocent human being is unjust to that human being. And the direct killing of an innocent human being *is* intrinsically unjust, as Pope John Paul II has had occasion to remind us. So anyone who acknowledges this truth cannot but affirm, as a moral principle, the right to life, though he needn't choose to put the matter in these terms.

So I think the key difference of principle between Christians and liberals is not whether we speak in terms of rights (though it is true that Christians need not speak in those terms); rather, the difference is in the moral content of their views (regardless of whether the Christian expresses those views in the language of rights).

I recognize, of course, that in the minds of many people an association (i.e., a weak psychological link) exists between the concept of rights and liberal possessive individualism. And the inflation of rights-claims that Dr. O'Donovan remarks on is hardly an illusion. So some account of it must be given. But I do not think she is correct to speak of an inflationary *logic* of rights-claims. As I have said, claims of rights —like, let me now add, claims of justice more generally—are either true or false; our goal is to affirm the claims that are true and deny the false ones. So, for example, we can and should affirm the right of the unborn not to be directly killed, and deny the alleged right to abortion.

In defending the concept of rights against Dr. O'Donovan's claim that it is an undesirable element of contemporary Christian moral discourse, I hope I have made it clear that I am only partly in disagreement with her. This should be evident in my affirmation of rights that liberals deny (e.g., the right to life) and my denial of alleged rights that liberals affirm (e.g., the right to abortion). But it should also be evident that, in my view, rights can never play the foundational role in Christian moral and political philosophy that they play in the liberal philosophy of atomistic or possessive individualism. Christians want to talk about lots of things in addition to rights: these include (1) norms and principles of justice that are not conveniently translated into the language of rights; (2) norms and principles of morality, including those of the common good, that go beyond the require-ments of justice and are not reducible to these requirements; (3) vir-tues, especially virtues that do not consist merely in, or are not merely instrumental to, respecting the rights of others; and (4) human goods, especially non-instrumental goods, including irreducibly social goods that fulfull persons in respect of their natural sociability.

I differ from Professor O'Donovan only in supposing that a certain measured rights-talk is consistent with sound theorizing about all these other moral realities and with their proper integration into our social practices.

Comments

Joan O'Donovan: It seems to me that we are moving beyond the proper conception of rights when we speak of people *having* rights. People *are* claims. The claim that a certain person *is* requires other people to do particular things. That claim is mediated by the command of Christ, the command of love. Everything that is done for another person is done for Christ and for the other person in Christ. The notion that a person *has* rights is not intrinsic to the language of justice, and the two are not convertible. I couldn't disagree more strongly with John Finnis's position that all statements about justice can be converted into statements about rights and vice versa. That is simply not the case. It may be that rights are indispensable tools in the legal field, but to bring them into essential theological and philosophical language about the community is to do what Wycliffe opposed the papal church for doing: bringing the tools of the institutions of fallen humanity into the most fundamental conceptions of what man was created to be. They are dispensations for sinful humanity, but theological language has to put them in that perspective.

Robert George: I don't think it's right to hear John Finnis to say that *all* claims of justice can be translated into the language of rights. I think his position is the same as mine, which is that all claims about rights can be translated into the language of justice. Some, but not all, claims about justice can conveniently be translated into the language of rights.

Paul Marshall: Joan O'Donovan just mentioned rights as a *legal* category. That rather than the ethical area is where I think they are

---

Note: The participants in this conversation are identified on pages 173-74.

162

important. Rights are what states establish, or what is constitu-
tionally established for them, to provide protection for citizens and
others. What we need to do is to provide good reasons why states
should establish rights and to spell out what rights should be included.

I think a lot of the impetus in both Catholic circles and Reformed
circles for wanting to stress a rights idea is tied to that legal side. What
people are interested in is the idea of a law-state, more than a notion
of subjective or natural rights per se. I'm not sure what "subjective
right" would mean. With a legal right, you're always specifying a
relationship between two or more things. To speak of a subjective
right necessarily gets hold of that relationship from only one end, and
sees it simply from one side.

Robert George: I picked up the term "subjective right" from Dr.
O'Donovan's paper. I take it to mean an individual right as opposed
to a communal right. I have no stake in that term or in defending a
concept of subjective right if it means that the content is loaded up
with the liberal agenda.

Paul Marshall: To speak of a relation as a right necessarily does that.
To speak of a right as something that a person *has* necessarily does
that, whether we use the term "subjective" or not.

Robert George: It seems to me there are only three options. (1) A
certain proposition is true, (2) it is false, or (3) it is incoherent or
effectively meaningless. Take this: either (1) the unborn have a right
not to be aborted, or (2) they don't have such a right, or (3) the
proposition "The unborn have a right not to be aborted" is not a
meaningful proposition.

Joan O'Donovan: It's a bad theological proposition. It's correct to
say that it is wrong to kill unborn fetuses, that it is unjust to kill unborn
fetuses, that Christ commands you not to kill unborn fetuses, and that
it's against the law of God to kill unborn fetuses, but not that fetuses
have rights.

Paul Marshall: That is what I would say as well.

Robert George: So it's a false proposition that the fetus has a right not to be killed?

Paul Marshall: It depends on what level you want to speak at. At a popular or rhetorical level I'm quite willing to use that language with a journalist.

Robert George: I'm not asking about what you would say to a journalist. I'm asking, is this a true proposition, a false proposition, or an incoherent or meaningless proposition?

Paul Marshall: I would say that if used precisely it's an incoherent proposition.

Russell Hittinger: Perhaps there's another aspect of this issue. I like the three options, but the proposition has to be materially true as well. For instance, if someone were to say, "Your life is not mine," he would be asserting a fact about the real world—"your life is not mine, it's yours." But I can say, "I can't take your life without doing an injustice to you," without implying that your life is your property, or that you *have* your life in the proprietary sense.

Robert George: That's an important point. Nothing in the proposition that says an unborn child has a right not to be aborted presupposes that an unborn child has, or that any of us has, a property of self-ownership. In fact, to get to the proposition that the unborn have a right to life I think you have to deny person-body dualism, which is exactly what's at stake. In any event, to make this claim about justice and translate it into the language of rights in no way implies any self-ownership.

Joan O'Donovan: My argument is that the use of the word "have" does imply self-ownership. I think you can say that the fetus *is* a right or *is* a claim as the object of God's love and care. As soon as you get into the language of having rights, you are into a language of proprietary subjectivity.

Robert George: Is that a logical claim you're making? Or is it a psychological claim? Why should I affirm it?

[margin handwritten note: a right to live suppose it would be unjust for God to "ordain death?"]

Joan O'Donovan: I think there are good empirical supports for it. The language of *having* rights is, in our time, highly determinative of people's ethical perspective. It seems to me that the quarrels about the rights of the fetus versus the rights of the mother have a kind of futility. If you go on using the language of rights, you're always going to elicit the response from the woman that she owns her own womb. The only possible way out of the impasse is to break through into the language of justice and law and goodness, a language that does not depend on or evoke the concept of proprietary rights.

John West: I want to add some additional weight to what Joan O'Donovan is saying but then come back and defend what Robby George is saying. It seems to me, Robby, that your main point is that modern rights-talk is not necessarily anti-Christian. While that might be true, I'm not sure it meets the full force of what Joan is talking about. When you get to the real world where human sinfulness comes into play, you might be able to make the argument that rights-talk, though it's not logically anti-Christian, for all practical purposes leads to the sort of modern perversity that we see at work in Dworkin and others. I think that's a stronger argument.

However, I dispute that. When Joan O'Donovan listed where the modern tradition of rights came from, she mentioned Hobbes and Locke, and then the theoretical exponents of the American and French Revolutions. As a historical matter, I would bring up the American Revolution. From the time of the American founding at least until the Civil War, you found rights-talk phrased in such a way that it was not at all incompatible with Christianity. In fact, Americans talking about natural rights often talked about being independent of all *but* the moral law or the law of God. It was independence vis-à-vis other human beings, but no human being had the right to rule over another tyrannically. This did not lead them to claim that they were not under sovereign moral laws, and it didn't disconnect them from talking about justice. In fact, when they talked about liberty, they usually distinguished it from license. In the state constitutions, and in the preambles to some of the bills of rights in state constitutions, they talked about why we were ordaining this government, why limited government is important, and they listed different virtues like temperance.

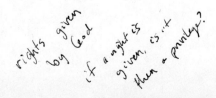

Robert George: A couple of important distinctions. First of all, to claim that propositions about rights are true is not to claim that every proposition about rights is true—or that when you have conflicting propositions about rights, both can't be either true or false. Second, when we do have conflicting claims of right, like the right of a woman to have an abortion and the right of the fetus not to be aborted, we're not going to be able to resolve that question and decide who really does have the right simply by using the language of rights. It is no part of my claim that rights language is all we have, or that it is sufficient to do the moral analysis that would enable us to conclude at the end of the day that thus-and-so proposition about a right holds, obtains, or is true.

Finally, it's not simply a historical matter. It's like the old line about the Maine farmer who was asked, "Do you believe in infant baptism?" His answer was, "Yeah, I've seen it done." Do I believe that the analysis of rights can be done without incorporating the liberal agenda? Well, yes, I've seen it done, in work by Pope John Paul II, Professor Hadley Arkes, and a lot of others.

John West: But politics is a realm of prudence, and if a case can be made that it tends to degenerate. . . . Is Hadley Arkes or Ronald Dworkin more influential in most law schools in this country?

Robert George: It doesn't have anything to do with the language.

John West: It does if your primary focus is public policy—how you get from here to there.

Robert George: If you want to say that, as a matter of prudence, we shouldn't use rights language, we'll have an argument about that and you might be right; I'm not dug in on this one. But if you want to say, as Joan O'Donovan does, that the language of rights builds in with this notion of having a right the very logic of possessive individualism, that's a much stronger and much more interesting claim. I don't think it's true, but if it is, it has big consequences.

David Smolin: I'd like to bring the conversation back to the broad theme of natural law. My first concern is that we have tried to make natural law do too many different things. We've talked about it in terms of how should Christians do moral theology, how Christians should do moral theology for the non-Christian, how Christians should think about their relationship with the non-Christian; we've talked about it in terms of how we govern with force, in terms of "the left hand of God." I don't think that Calvin, Luther, or the Catholic Church expected natural law to do so many different things for them —how to deal with the Turks, how to deal with one another.

It seems to me that creation-talk can carry more weight in the current culture and is a necessary corrective to rights-talk. Creation-talk contradicts the misunderstanding of natural law by which it gets changed into natural rights. It brings us back to the creation account and helps us do moral theology. We're not in Jerusalem; we're in Athens. The Athenians don't understand creation, and we need to begin there.

Robert George: What I said about rights I would also say about the more fundamental principles of the natural law. I'm not at all happy with the idea of "using" natural law as if it were some sort of an instrument. The claims about those more fundamental propositions that constitute the natural law are either true or false. If they're true, we must affirm them; if they're false, we shouldn't affirm them. It's not as if we had an option in some abstract sense of using them or not using them. We act on those principles all the time.

James Schall: Maitain said in *Man and the State* that we should stop using the word "sovereignty" in politics because it's really a theological word. Allan Bloom said in *The Closing of the American Mind* that we should stop using the word "value." It's a Max Weber word and it's a dangerous word. The Pope, alas, uses it all the time. I think we should get rid of "rights" also, but I acknowledge Robby George's point that it's a prudential thing.

I think Hobbes was the one who said that there is such a thing as a "right" with no relationship to anything other than one's claim to whatever he wants. The first time that "right" was moved to the subjective side was with Suárez. At that point it stopped being this *ius*, this objective relationship that stood between us, and became something of a claim on my side with no objective referent.

Russell Hittinger: I want to return to an important concept that I think can affect how you regard rights, both legally and morally. To say that something has inherent value does not mean that it's an end in itself simply speaking. The traditional doctrine, or at least one traditional doctrine, was that the whole genus of ethics is action as ordered to an ultimate end, and that there could be no ultimate end other than God, though there are questions to ask about differences between nature and grace in attending to that end. Human beings have inherent value, but by nature they're ordered to something other than themselves, and that's not just other people laterally.

Once you relocate your perspective in the older tradition, I do believe that the ontology of rights becomes more difficult. If by nature it is true that men do not belong to themselves, here is the ontological question: Can we reconcile the moral language of rights with the notion that human beings are by nature, not just by supernature, ordained to God as their ultimate end?

Robert Tuttle: Let me go back to a point about the separation of use and dominion and consider the matter of trusteeship. I think C. B. Macpherson misreads Locke significantly on this point—in fact, butchers Locke. Locke doesn't have a sense of self-ownership at all. One does not own oneself; one owns only as a trustee for God. The sense of rights as being proprietary, as subjective in the sense that you own yourself and therefore that self is distanced from God, doesn't explain this whole early part of the tradition, nor does it take adequate account of the Lutheran understanding of the orders of creation. You stand as a trustee of God for yourself, exercising control in a sense, exercising responsibility for using the gifts of creation toward their proper end.

We can talk about a fetus having a "right to life" in the sense that we can somehow impute to all others the responsibility of trusteeship. The fetus can't speak for itself; we have to speak for it. In order to exercise its destiny, for the sake of its life with God, the fetus needs to be born. I think the sense that all rights language must necessarily be subjective, in the sense of detached from a relationship with God, is a misreading of the early part of the tradition.

Luis Lugo: There's a very similar argument in *Evangelium Vitae* on the use of physical things. The idea of dominion is clearly linked to trusteeship when John Paul speaks about our use of created things.

Keith Pavlischek: I'd like to try to tie together the notion of natural law and proprietary rights by asking about how we understand the right to religious freedom. St. Thomas understands religion as a species of the natural virtue of justice. Religion is an obligation: it is what we owe to God. Now, how does this relate to the civil right of religious freedom, my right to worship any way that I want, whether to take part in a Wiccan ceremony or to play golf on Sunday morning rather than go to church? The question arises: is this civil right also a human right? If you understand religion as an obligation one has to God, a requirement of the natural law, it is hard to see how failing one's obligation can be a human right that one "possesses." St. Thomas seems to say that if you don't render due homage to God, if you don't render the appropriate acknowledgment of God and his sovereignty, it is a violation of the natural law. But how can a violation of the natural law be a natural or human right? So, how does the idea of "possessive right" deal with the notion that I may have a civil right to play golf rather than worship on Sunday morning, but exercising that right is a violation of natural law?

Carl Henry: Why not say candidly that in the Judeo-Christian Scriptures there is no concept of authentic human rights grounded in the self or the community or the state, but that legitimate rights are only the flip side of divine duties and imperatives? While I wouldn't want to repeal the U.N. Declaration, nevertheless I would not want to justify it in terms of an essentially "rights" argument.

Robert George: Any doctrine of rights I would subscribe to would have as its underlying philosophy a natural law theory outside the liberal tradition. That natural law theory takes as the starting point of all practical thinking ends or purposes that are rationally desirable, not merely as means to other ends but as ends in themselves. They are rationally desirable for their own sake.

What is to be said in defense of my underlying philosophy? Nothing, I think, that has any particular bearing on the problem of rights.

So I think I can lay aside any discussion of rights at this point. I would only say this, that all of us do, effortlessly and often, act on prescriptive principles that direct us to do certain things as worthwhile, whether we like it or not. We're here today pursuing a certain form of knowledge, for example, on the understanding that knowledge is a worthwhile end. Some of us might have purely instrumental purposes in mind—we might get a publishable paper out of this, which will get us a raise at next year's salary review time, and so forth—but I suspect that most of us would consider the knowledge of the truth of the matters we are pursuing to be worthwhile for its own sake. It provides an intelligible reason for our deciding to put the effort into reading papers and writing papers and debating with one another, regardless of what additional value we might be able to derive.

I think the question Russ Hittinger wants to ask, though, is, "Can we really stop there? Or needn't we, at least as Christians, push the matter back a step, so that we say that the ultimate intelligibility rests not in the value of knowledge itself but in the ordering of that value and all other values to God?" Have I got the question right?

Russell Hittinger: Close to it.

Robert George: I want to affirm that people are ordered to God. It seems to me that the old-fashioned line is the correct one, that we were made to know God, to love and serve God in this world and the next. But I would not draw any sort of a sharp line between knowing, loving, and serving God and acting on principles that enable us to realize, for ourselves as individuals and for the communities we together constitute, the goods of human life. It seems to me that those are largely co-extensive, although the goods don't exhaust God. That is what is affirmed in *Gaudium et Spes*.

Is it true that, as someone said earlier, the life of the unborn child can be ordered only to God? I think the answer would be yes and no. If we distinguish God from the goods of this world sharply, then we have to say yes, because the goods of this world are genuinely goods, and will be recovered in the heavenly kingdom. But if we don't draw so sharp a distinction, then the answer is no. In preparing that child for a life of knowledge, of friendship, a life in which he is fulfilled in the goods available to him by his free action and thus his participation in the eternal law and the providential plan, we are ordering the child to God.

On the question of trusteeship: First, because I don't want to spout heresy, let me just ask whether the Church teaches us that God owns us. I think not, because he has made us sons and not slaves.

Paul Marshall: It's Locke who teaches that God owns us.

Robert George: Exactly, and this is what I want to say in response to Locke. What are before us in the liberal tradition are false options. The liberal says, Either you own yourself, or the state owns you, or God owns you. To say God owns you is the way out of saying that the state owns you or you own yourself. But those are false options. The reality is that we human beings are the sorts of things that can't be owned. We're not commodities. The question "Who owns you?" is not a coherent or meaningful question. Human beings "have" interests and rights (such as the human right not to be enslaved), but this "having" in no way implies self-ownership. This is why we "have," in addition to interests and rights, moral reponsibilities, even in regard to our own putatively self-regarding actions.

Russell Hittinger: On this point, Robby, you don't have a strong enough sense of final causality. There is a difference but no contra-diction between saying that (1) I have an obligation, by nature and not just by divine revelation, to love God above all else and to love all other creatures, and saying that (2) insofar as those are other human beings like myself, I have an obligation to love them as something more than instruments. There's no contradiction in saying that all human beings are by nature ordered to God as the final cause, and saying they're not mere instruments either. That's precisely what it means to love them.

Robert George: On this point, at least, Russ, we are in "heated agreement."

Conference Participants

Carl E. Braaten, executive director, Center for Catholic and Evangelical Theology, Northfield, Minn.

David Coffin, pastor, New Hope Presbyterian Church, Fairfax, Va.

Charles Colson, chairman, Prison Fellowship Ministries, Reston, Va.

Alan Crippen, senior fellow, Institute for Family Studies, Focus on the Family, Colorado Springs, Colo.

Michael Cromartie, senior fellow, Ethics and Public Policy Center, Washington, D.C.

William Edgar, professor of apologetics, Westminster Theological Seminary, Philadelphia.

Robert P. George, professor of politics, Princeton University, Princeton, N.J.

Timothy George, dean, Beeson Divinity School, Birmingham, Ala.

Carl F. H. Henry, visiting scholar, Trinity Evangelical Divinity School, Deerfield, Ill.

Russell Hittinger, Warren Professor of Catholic Studies, University of Tulsa, Tulsa, Okla.

Deal Hudson, editor, *Crisis* magazine, Washington, D.C.

Luis Lugo, professor of political science, Calvin College, Grand Rapids, Mich., and Center for Public Justice.

Paul Marshall, senior member in political theory, Institute for Christian Studies, Toronto, Ontario.

Joan Lockwood O'Donovan, writer and lecturer, Oxford, England.

Keith Pavlischek, director, Crossroads Program, Evangelicals for Social Action, Wynnewood, Pa.

Nancy Pearcey, policy director, The Wilberforce Forum, Prison Fellowship Ministries, Reston, Va.

Robert Royal, vice president, Ethics and Public Policy Center, Washington, D.C.

James Schall, S.J., professor of government, Georgetown University, Washington, D.C.

Susan E. Schreiner, professor of church history, University of Chicago.

James Skillen, executive director, Center for Public Justice, Annapolis, Md.

David Smolin, professor of law, Cumberland School of Law, Samford University, Birmingham, Ala.

Robert Tuttle, associate professor of law, George Washington University, Washington, D.C.

Michael Uhlmann, senior fellow, Ethics and Public Policy Center, Washington, D.C.

John West, senior fellow, The Discovery Institute, Seattle, Wash., and Seattle Pacific University.

Daniel Westberg, assistant professor of religious studies, University of Virginia, Charlottesville.

Notes

CHAPTER 1
"Natural Law and Catholic Moral Theology"
RUSSELL HITTINGER

1. Yves R. Simon, *The Tradition of Natural Law: A Philosopher's Reflections,* ed. Vukan Kuic, intro. Russell Hittinger (New York: Fordham University Press, 1992 reprint, orig. 1965), 5.

2. Thanks to Steve Long, Robert Tuttle, and Keith Pavlischek, who made useful suggestions and criticisms of earlier drafts of this paper.

3. *Church Dog.* II/1, §36.

4. *Adv. Judaeos,* cap. 2 (PL 2-2, 599, 600), *quasi matrix omnium praeceptorum Dei. . . . non scriptam, quae naturaliter intelligebatur.*

5. A millennium later, Thomas Aquinas would also refer to the time between the Fall and the Law as the time of the law of nature, when God left men to what little they could glean from the original law in order to curb their pride (*S.t.* I-II, q. 98, a. 6). As for who knew and abided by the natural law, Thomas says the patriarchs, who were men of faith. Commenting on the figurative meaning of the sacrifices in the Jewish ceremonies, Thomas tries to draw together the phases of revelation in Christology:

> The figurative cause is that the bread signifies Christ Who is the *panis vivus* [living bread], as stated in Jn. 6. He was indeed an ear of corn, as it were, during the state of the law of nature, and in the faith of the patriarchs; he was like flour in the doctrine of the Law of the prophets; and he was like perfect bread after he had taken human nature; baked in the fire, that is, formed by the Holy Spirit in the oven of the virginal womb; baked again in a pan by the toils which he suffered in the world; and consumed by fire on the cross as on a gridiron. [*S.t.* I-II, q. 102, a. 3, ad 12]

For Thomas's estimation of Abraham, see note 20.

6. Gregory of Nyssa, *The Life of Moses,* transl., intro., and notes by Abraham J. Malherbe and Everett Ferguson (New York: Paulist Press, 1978), II §215-16.

7. Note the similarity to Thomas's formulation of the first precept of law in *S.t.* I-II, 94.2—*Bonum est faciendum et prosequendum, et malum vitandum,* the good is to be

done and pursued, and evil resisted. Thomas calls it the *primum praeceptum legis,* the first precept of law.

8. Regarding debates *ad extra,* the patristic theologians tend to worry about rival Jewish or Gnostic accounts of divine governance. Gnostics asserted that the "law" in Gen. 2.17 was a dietary (and hence a positive) law of the Demiurge, the same deity that shows up later in Jewish scriptures giving more positive (and usually dietary) laws. Against the rabbis, Christian apologists contended not only that there is law after the Mosaic law, but that the *lex nova* restores a law antecedent to Sinai.

9. . . . *per primam Dei gratiam, id est per legem naturae.* Denz. 336.

10. *Instit. Justin.* I.2.

11. Ibid. I.2.3.

12. Ibid. IV.18.4.

13. *Decretum Gratiani* I.D.1, can. 3, 4.

14. *S.t.* I-II, q. 91.

15. The new Catechism of the Catholic Church gathers all law together under the rubric "moral law," the various species designating modes of divine pedagogy. CCC §1950-52.

16. *S.t.* I-II, q. 91, a. 2, ad 1.

17. It is an understandable but regrettable mistake to focus exclusively on *S.t.* I-II, q. 94. Here, indeed, Thomas speaks of natural law in terms of what is first in the mind and first in nature. He makes no reference to God. But in q. 94 he is not defining the natural law; the *ratio formalis*—what it is, and what makes it law—is discussed in qq. 91 and 93. Question 94 takes up the *ratio materialis:* natural law as an effect in the creature.

18. *S.t.* I-II, q. 93, a. 2.

19. *S.t.* I-II, q. 90, a. 4, ad 1.

20. In II Rom., lectio 3 (§215-216). St. Thomas notes that unless we distinguish between the two classes of gentiles, Rom. 2.14 would be open to a Pelagian reading of these two words *naturaliter* and *faciunt.* In *S.t.* III, 1.6, St. Thomas contends that the election of Abraham and the dispensation of the law to Moses presupposed the restoration of knowledge of the sovereign of the natural law: "He was pleased to choose Abraham as a standard of the restored knowledge of God and of holy living [*in quo forma esset renovatae notitiae Dei et morum*]."

21. *S.t.* I, q. 1, a. 1.

22. *S.t.* II-II, q. 94, a. 1.

23. Thomas Aquinas, *Collationes in Decem Praeceptis,* I, line 27, édition critique avec introduction et notes par Jean-Pierre Torrell, in *Revue des Sciences philosophiques et théologiques* 69 (1985): 5-40, 227-63.

24. *S.t.* I-II, q. 97, a. 1, ad 1.

25. *S.t.* I-II, q. 89, a. 6.

26. *S.t.* I-II, q. 98, a. 6.

27. Thomas Hobbes, *De Homine,* X.5.

28. *Flumina honestatis redeunt ad mare iuris naturalis, quod ita processit, ut quod in primo homine pene perditum est, in lege mosayca relevaretur, in evangelio perficeretur, in moribus decoraretur.* Johannes Faventinus, *Summa,* Brit. Mus., MS Royal 9 E. vii, fol. 2, c. 2.

29. For example, *Diuturnum,* issued on June 29, 1881, three months after the assassination of the Russian czar Alexander II, who was killed on the very day that

he signed a new liberal constitution, directly criticizes the secular ideologies of natural law.

30. Cardinal Maurice Roy, "Occasion of the Tenth Anniversary of the Encyclical *Pacem in Terris*" (April 11, 1973), #128. In Joseph Gremillion, *The Gospel of Peace and Justice* (New York: Orbis Books, 1976), 557.

31. *Pacem in Terris*, §1.

32. Yves Simon was a conspicuous exception. He worried that the problem of natural law in our times is not so much the need to defend the idea against its cultured critics, but rather to prevent it from being ensconced in ideologies formed under the practical pressure of responding to the various intellectual and institutional felonies of modern life.

> Our time has witnessed a new birth of belief in natural law concomitantly with the success of existentialism, which represents the most thorough criticism of natural law ever voiced by philosophers. Against such powers of destruction we feel the need for an ideology of natural law. The current interest in this subject certainly expresses an aspiration of our society at a time when the foundations of common life and of just relations are subjected to radical threats. No matter how sound these aspirations may be, they are quite likely to distort philosophic treatments. For a number of years we have been witnessing a tendency, in teachers and preachers, to assume that natural law decides, with the universality proper to the necessity of essences, incomparably more issues than it is actually able to decide. There is a tendency to treat in terms of natural law questions which call for treatment in terms of prudence. It should be clear that any concession to this tendency is bound promptly to cause disappointment and skepticism. [Simon, *The Tradition of Natural Law*, 23]

33. Joseph Cardinal Bernardin, "Seeking a Common Ground on Human Rights," *Depaul Law Review* 36 (1987): 159-65.

34. *Evangelium Vitae*, §18.

35. Ibid.

36. Servais Pinckaers, O.P., *The Sources of Christian Ethics*, trans. Sr. Mary Thomas Noble, O.P. (Washington D.C.: The Catholic University of America Press, 1995), 298-99.

37. Josef Fuchs, *Moral Demands and Personal Obligations*, trans. Brian McNeil (Washington, D.C.: Georgetown University Press, 1993), 100.

38. Ibid., 55.

39. The majority of Paul VI's Commission for the Study of Problems of the Family, Population, and Birth Rate issued a report urging that the Church change its teaching on contraception. The authors of the majority report at least had the honesty to state their theological premise clearly. They reasoned that although the sources of human life are from created nature, the rules for the choice and administration of that natural value fall to human jurisdiction. "To take his own or another's life is a sin," the Majority Report contended, "not because life is under the exclusive dominion of God but because it is contrary to right reason unless there is question of a good or a higher order."

40. Fuchs, *Moral Demands*, 39.

41. The encyclical says,

> Deep within his conscience man discovers a law which he has not laid upon himself but which he must obey. Its voice, ever calling him to love and to do what

is good and to avoid evil, tells him inwardly at the right moment: do this, shun that. For man has in his heart a law inscribed by God. His dignity lies in observing this law, and by it he will be judged. His conscience is man's most secret core, and his sanctuary. There he is alone with God whose voice echoes in his depths. [GS §16]

42. Fuchs, *Moral Demands,* 157.

43. Ibid., 40.

44. *Veritatis Splendor* (VS) §4.

45. The subtitle reads: *De Fundamentis Doctrinae Moralis Ecclesiae,* "Concerning the Foundations of the Church's Moral Teaching."

46. VS §4.

47. VS §37.

48. VS §40.

49. VS §74.

50. Ibid.

51. VS §29.

52. John Calvin, *Institutes of the Christian Religion,* trans. John Allen, 2 vols. (Philadelphia: Presbyterian Board of Christian Education, 1936), I. ii.1, 270.

53. VS §11.

54. VS §13.

55. VS §9. See Karol Wojtyla: "For 'a religious man' means not so much 'one who is capable of religious experiences' (as is generally supposed) as above all 'one who is just to God the Creator'" (Karol Wojtyla, *Love and Responsibility,* trans. H. T. Willetts [San Francisco: Ignatius Press, 1981], 223).

56. Georges Cottier, O.P., "Morality of a human act depends primarily on object chosen by will" (*L'Osservatore Romano* no. 6 (February 9, 1994): 11).

57. E.g., in *Laborem Exercens* and *Evangelium Vitae.*

58. VS §36.

59. VS §41.

60. In scholastic parlance, the human reason is a measuring measure *(mensura mensurans)* only insofar as it is first a measured measure *(mensura mensurata).*

61. "Others speak, and rightly so, of theonomy, or participated theonomy, since man's free obedience to God's law effectively implies that human reason and human will participate in God's wisdom and providence" (VS §41).

62. VS §2.

63. VS §12,46.

64. VS §38.

65. VS §58.

66. "The judgment of conscience does not establish the law; rather it bears witness to the authority of the natural law and of the practical reason with reference to the supreme good, whose attractiveness the human person perceives and whose commandments he accepts" (VS §60).

67. VS §45.

68. In the *London Tablet* Bernard Haring rejected the papal encyclical *Veritatis Splendor,* basing his objection (in part) on a right of conscience grounded in natural law. See *National Catholic Reporter,* November 5, 1993.

69. VS §86.
70. VS §103.
71. *Church Dog.* II/1, §36, "Ethics as a Task of the Doctrine of God," 527.
72. On the new catechism see note 15.
73. John Courtney Murray, S.J., *We Hold These Truths* (New York: Image Book edition, 1964), 53.
74. Sen. Joseph Biden, "Law and Natural Law," *Washington Post,* September 8, 1991. Senator Biden, it may be recalled, voted against the confirmation of Robert Bork because, among other reasons, Bork expressly rejected judicial uses of natural law. Against Bork, Biden declared: "I have certain inalienable rights because I exist."

CHAPTER 2

"Calvin's Use of Natural Law"

SUSAN E. SCHREINER

1. The following survey of secondary scholarship is dependent on Arthur C. Cochrane, "Natural Law in Calvin," in Elwyn A. Smith, ed., *Church-State Relations in Ecumenical Perspective* (Louvain: Duquesne University Press, 1966), 176-217, and William Klempa, "Calvin on Natural Law," in Timothy George, ed., *John Calvin and the Church: A Prism of Reform* (Louisville: Westminster/John Knox Press, 1990), 72-95.
2. August Lang, *Die Reformation und das Naturrecht* (Gütersloh, 1909), 18-20.
3. Gisbert Beyerhaus, *Studien zur Staatsanschauung Calvins* (1910).
4. Ernst Troeltsch, *The Social Teachings of the Christian Churches,* tr. Olive Wyon (New York: Macmillan, 1949) 2:897.
5. Ibid.
6. Ernst Troeltsch, "Calvin and Calvinism," *Hibbert Journal* 8 (1909): 116f.
7. Émile Doumergue, *Jean Calvin—Les hommes et les choses de son temps,* 7 vols. (Lausanne: G. Bridel et Cie, 1897-1917) 5:465-70, 580.
8. Josef Bohatec, *Calvin und das Recht* (Feudingen: Buchdruck und Verlags-Anstalt, 1934).
9. Emil Brunner and Karl Barth, *Natural Theology* ("Nature and Grace" by Brunner and the Reply "No!" by Barth), tr. P. Fraenkel (London: Geoffrey Bles, Centenary Press, 1946), 37.
10. Cochrane, "Natural Law in Calvin," 177.
11. Brunner, "Nature and Grace," in *Natural Theology,* 37.
12. Ibid.
13. Ibid., 38.
14. Ibid., 42f.
15. Ibid., 106.
16. Ibid.
17. Ibid., 109.
18. Günter Gloede, *Theologia Naturalis bei Calvin* (Stuttgart: W. Kohlhammer, 1935).
19. Peter Brunner, "Allgemeine und besondere Offenbarung in Calvins Institu-

tio," in *Evangelische Theologie*, 1/5 (August 1934): 189-215. Peter Barth, "Das Problem der natürlichen Theologie bei Calvin," *Theologische Existenz Heute*, no. 18 (Munich: Chr. Kaiser, 1935); Wilhelm Niesel, *The Theology of Calvin* (Philadelphia: Westminster Press, 1956).

20. Edward A. Dowey, *The Knowledge of God in Calvin's Theology* (New York: Columbia University Press, 1952).

21. T. H. L. Parker, *Calvin's Doctrine of the Knowledge of God*, 2d. ed. (Edinburgh: Oliver and Boyd, 1969). The reader should take note of two other important studies from this period that discuss Calvin's view of natural law: Marc-Édouard Chenevière, *La pensée politique de Calvin* (Geneva: Éditions Labor et Fides, 1937), and John T. McNeill, "Natural Law in the Teaching of the Reformers," *Journal of Religion* 26 (1946): 168-82.

22. Cochrane, "Natural Law in Calvin," 181.

23. David Little, "Calvin and the Prospects for a Christian Theory of Natural Law," in Gene H. Outka and Paul Ramsey, ed., *Norm and Context in Christian Ethics* (New York: Scribner's, 1968), 175-97. See also David Little, "Natural Law Revisited: James Luther Adams and Beyond," *Union Seminary Quarterly Review* 37 (1982): 217-18. In the latter essay Little stresses that members of all religious traditions have a crucial stake in natural law thinking. The conviction that there is a knowledge of natural law means that the law of nature is based on the conviction that there is something prior to and beyond revelation that provides the basis for morality.

24. William J. Bouwsma, *John Calvin: A Sixteenth-Century Portrait* (New York and Oxford: Oxford University Press, 1988), 73-76, 166-67.

25. William Klempa, "Calvin on Natural Law," in George, ed., *John Calvin and the Church*, 89.

26. McNeill, "Natural Law in the Teaching of the Reformers," 168.

27. *Inst.* II.8.1.

28. Comm. on Rom. 2:14, in T. H. L. Parker, ed, *Iohannis Calvini Commentarius in Epistolam Pauli ad Romanos,* vol. 22 of Studies in the History of Christian Thought (Leiden: E. J. Brill, 1981), 45.

29. Ibid., 45-46.

30. *Inst.* IV.20.16.

31. CO 27:568.

32. *Inst.* II.8.1.

33. *Inst.* II.1.7.

34. *Inst.* II.2.12. The distinction regarding the effect of sin on the supernatural and natural gifts dates from Lombard (*Sentences* II.xxv.8). See also Augustine, *On Nature and Grace* III.3, XIX.21, XX.22., and *Questions on the Gospels* II.9.

35. Barth, "No! Answer to Emil Brunner," in *Natural Theology*, 79.

36. *Inst.* IV.10.3 (my emphasis).

37. *Inst.* II.2.22.

38. *Inst.* I.15.4. In *Inst.* I.15.3 Calvin describes the original image of God in terms of an original created order:

Therefore, although the soul is not man, yet it is not absurd for man, in respect to his soul, to be called God's image; even though I retain the principle I just now set forward, that the likeness of God extends to the whole excellence by which man's nature towers over all the kinds of living creatures. Accordingly, the integrity with which Adam was endowed is expressed by this word when he had full possession of right understanding, when he had his affections kept within the bounds of reason, all his senses tempered in right order, and he truly referred his excellence to unexceptional gifts bestowed upon him by his Maker. And although the primary seat of the divine image was in the mind and heart, or in the soul and its powers, yet there was no part of man, not even the body itself, in which some sparks did not glow.

39. *Inst.* II.2.12.

40. CO 47:9, Comm. on John 1:9.

41. Barth, "No! Answer to Emil Brunner," in *Natural Theology*, 74.

42. *Inst.* II.8.11.

43. *Inst.* II.2.24.

44. On Calvin's doctrine of providence see Josef Bohatec, "Calvins Vorse-hungslehre," in *Calvinstudien: Festschrift zum 400. Geburtstage Johann Calvins* (Leipzig: Rudolf Haupt, 1909); Henri Strohl, "La pensée de Calvin sur la providence divine au temps ou il était réfugié à Strasbourg," *Revue d'histoire et de philosophie religieuses* 22 (1942): 154-69. For an expanded discussion of the following sections see Susan E. Schreiner, *The Theater of His Glory: John Calvin and the Natural Order* (Durham, N.C.: Labyrinth Press, 1991; repr. by Baker Book House, 1995).

45. CO 23:16, Comm. on Gen. 1:2. See also CO 21:42-43, Comm. on Nahum 1:5; CO 38:376, Sermon on Deut. 5:9-14. Werner Krusche, *Das Wirken des Heiligen Geistes nach Calvin* (Göttingen: Vandenhoek and Ruprecht, 1957), 15ff.

46. See also Günter Gloede, *Theologia naturalis bei Calvin*, 332-34; Benjamin Charles Milner, *Calvin's Doctrine of the Church* (Leiden: E. J. Brill, 1970), 1-25; Melanchthon, *Initia doctrinae physicae*, CR 13:200; idem, *Loci praecipui theologici*, 1559, MW II/220-21.

47. *Inst.* I.5.2; I.14.21. Cf. Cicero, *De natura deorum*, II.15-17; Seneca, *De providentia*, I.2-5; Chrysostom, *Ad eos qui scandalizati sunt*, VII.1ff.

48. *Inst.* I.14.1. See also CO 37:180, Comm. on Isa. 48:13; and Pierre Duhem, *Le système du monde: Histoire des doctrines cosmologiques de Platon a Copernic* (Paris: Hermann, 1958), IX:88.

49. CO 37:631-32, Comm. on Jer. 5:22. See also CO 31:328, Comm. on Ps. 33:7:

> The Psalmist celebrates a signal and remarkable miracle which we see in looking on the surface of the earth; namely, that God gathers together the element of water, fluid and unstable as it is, into a solid heap and holds it so at his pleasure. . . . In this we certainly perceive that God, who is always attentive to the welfare of the human race, has enclosed the waters within certain invisible barriers and keeps them shut up to this day; the prophet elegantly declares that they stand still at God's commandment as if they were a heap of firm and solid matter.

See also Richard Stauffer, *Dieu, la création et la providence dans la prédication de Calvin* (Berne: Peter Lang, 1978), 186-87.

50. CO 23:131-132, Comm. on Gen. 7:11.

51. CO 23:19, Comm. on Gen. 1:9.

52. CO 32:86-87, Comm. on Ps. 104:5

53. CO 35:366-67, Sermon on Job 38:2-10.

54. CO 32:620, Sermon on Ps. 119.

55. CO 23:55, Comm. on Gen. 3:1.

56. Ibid.

57. CO 37:635, Comm. on Jer. 5:25. See also CO 36:402, Comm. on Isa. 24:5-6; CO 31:94, Comm. on Ps. 8:7; CO 23:40, Comm. on Gen. 2:10; and Arnold Williams, *The Common Expositor: An Account of the Commentaries on Genesis, 1527-1663* (Chapel Hill: University of North Carolina Press, 1948).

58. Comm. on Rom. 8:20, in Parker, ed., *Iohannis Calvini Commentarius*.

59. CO 33:57, CO 34:220, CO 35:171, Sermons on Job 1:6-8, 21:7-12, 24:21-26; CO 51:457, Sermon on Eph. 3:7-9; CO 31:361-62, Comm. on Ps. 36:6.

60. CO 31:167, Comm. on Ps. 17:15; CO 36:581, 585-86, Comm. on Isa. 34:4; CO 33:450-51, Sermon on Job 9:23-28. On Calvin's view of history see: Heinrich Berger, *Calvins Geschichtsauffassung* (Zurich: Zwingli-Verlag, 1955); Bohatec, *Budé und Calvin: Studien zur Gedankenwelt des französischen Frühhumanismus* (Graz: Böhlau, 1950), 280-300; idem, "Gott und die Geschichte nach Calvin," *Philosophia Reformata* (1936): 129-61; Charles Trinkaus, "Renaissance Problems in Calvin's Theology," in W. Peery, ed., *Studies in the Renaissance* (Austin: University of Texas Press, 1954) I:59-80.

61. CO 33:403, Sermon on Job 8:13-32; CO 23:143-144, Comm. on Gen. 9:2; CO 33:275-276, Sermon on Job 5:19-27; CO 34:243, Sermon on Job 21:16-21; CO 35:462, Sermon on Job 40:7-19; CO 35:145, Sermon on Job 37:7-13.

62. *Inst.* I.14.17; I.17.11; CO 33:57-69, Sermon on Job 1:6-8.

63. *Inst.* I.18.1-2. Cf. *Inst.* II.4.3 and III.23.8.

64. *Inst.* IV.20.16. On the role of the conscience in Calvin's thought see M. E. Chenevière, *La pensée politique de Calvin* (Geneva: Editions Labor et Fides, 1937), 46ff.; Bohatec, *Budé und Calvin*, 384-85; David Lee Foxgrover, "John Calvin's Understanding of the Conscience" (Ph.D dissertation, Claremont Graduate School, 1978); Gloede, *Theologia naturalis bei Calvin*, 103-34; Peter Pelkonen, "The Teaching of John Calvin on the Nature and Function of the Conscience," *Lutheran Quarterly* 21 (1969): 77-88; J. Baur, *Gott, Recht und weltliches Regiment im Werke Calvins*, 46-49; and Ronald Wallace, *Calvin's Doctrine of the Christian Life* (Edinburgh and London: Oliver and Boyd, 1959), 141-47.

65. *Inst.* IV.20.16.

66. CO 33:489, Sermon on Job 10:7-15: ". . . l'image de Dieu est imprimee en nous, d'autant que avons intelligence et raison, que nous discernons entre le bien et le mal, que les homnes sont nais pour avoir quelque ordre, quelque police entre eux: qu'un chacun a sa conscience qui lui rend tesmoignage que cela est mauvais que cela est bon." See also CO 35:238-39, Sermon on Job 35:8-11.

67. CO 23: 96-97, Comm. on Gen. 4:15; CO 24:611-112, Harmony of the Five Books of Moses, Exod. 20:13; *Supplementa Calviniana* I:95ff, Sermon on II Sam. 4:11-12.

68. CO 23:495, Comm. on Gen. 38:8.

69. CO 24:679, Harmony of the Five Books of Moses, Exod. 22:25.

70. *Inst.* II.2.13. Calvin, of course, attributed the origin of these natural instincts and universal impressions to God.

71. CO 23: 46-47, Comm. on Gen. 2:18; CO 52:277, Comm. on I Tim. 2:13.

72. CO 23:362-363, Comm. on Gen. 26:16.

73. CO 51:759, 762, Sermon on Eph. 5:28-30.

74. CO 24: 648, Comm. on Deut. 22:22.

75. C0 23:433, 499, Comm. on Gen. 31:50, 38:24.
76. CO 23:500, Comm. on Gen. 38:26; CO 24:661-62, Harmony of the Five Books of Moses, Lev. 18:6; *Supplementa Calviniana* I:358, 585-86, Sermon on II Sam. 20:2-10.
77. CO 24:662, Harmony of the Five Books of Moses, Lev. 18:6; CO 28:61, 63, Sermon on Deut 22:25-30.
78. CO 24:662-63, Harmony of the Five Books of Moses, Lev. 18:6.
79. CO 52:309, Comm. on 1 Tim. 5:8; CO 49:425, Comm. on I Cor. 7:37; CO 24:602-3, Harmony of the Five Books of Moses, Exod. 20:12; CO 27:686-87, Sermon on Deut. 21:18-21; CO 51:774, 788, Sermon on Eph. 5:31, 33, 6:1-4.
80. *Inst.* II.2.15.
81. *Inst.* IV.20.8.
82. CO 36:82, Comm. on Isa. 3:4.
83. *Inst.* IV.20.24.
84. *Inst.* IV.20.14.
85. CO 7:87 ff,, "Brieve instruction pour armer tous bons fideles contre les erreurs de la secte commune des Anabaptistes"; CO 7:103, 214-20, "Contre la secte phantastique et furieuse des Libertins"; CO 31:698, Comm. on Ps. 74:17.
86. CO 27:566, Sermon on Deut. 19:14-15.
87. Ibid.
88. CO 27:563-64, Sermon on Deut. 19:8-13; CO 27:588, Sermon on Deut. 19:16-21; CO 28:236-37, Sermon on Deut. 25:13-19; CO 24:675, Harmony of the Five Books of Moses, Lev. 19:35.
89. The phrase comes from David C. Steinmetz, *Luther in Context* (Bloomington: Indiana University Press, 1986), 96.
90. One of the best books on this topic is Zachary Sayre Schiffman, *On the Threshold of Modernity* (Baltimore and London: Johns Hopkins University Press, 1991).

TIMOTHY GEORGE

1. James D. Smart, ed., *Revolutionary Theology in the Making: Barth-Thurneysen Correspondence, 1914-1925* (Richmond: John Knox Press, 1964), 101.
2. John H. Leith, ed., *Creeds of the Churches* (Atlanta: John Knox Press, 1982), 520.
3. *Johannis Calvini Opera Selecta,* ed. Peter Barth and Wilhelm Niesel (Munich, 1926-36), 1:62.
4. Comm. on Deut. 22:22, quoted in Hans Hopfl, *The Christian Polity of John Calvin* (Cambridge: Cambridge University Press, 1982), 183.

CHAPTER 3
"The Reformed Tradition and Natural Law
DANIEL WESTBERG

1. Ian T. Ramsey, "Towards a Rehabilitation of Natural Law," in Ramsey, ed., *Christian Ethics and Contemporary Philosophy* (London: 1966), 382-96; and "Rethinking

Natural Law," in John Macquarrie, ed., *Three Issues in Ethics* (New York: Macmillan, 1970), chap. 4. For a recent and more reserved view see Carl Braaten, "Protestants and Natural Law," *First Things,* January 1992, 20, 23.

2. See John T. McNeill, "Natural Law in the Teaching of the Reformers," *Journal of Religion* 26 (1946): 168-82; David Little, "Calvin and the Prospects for a Christian Theory of Natural Law," in Gene W. Outka and Paul Ramsey, ed., *Norm and Context in Christian Ethics* (London: Scribner's, 1968).

3. Helmut Thielicke, *Theological Ethics* (Philadelphia: Fortress Press, 1966): 392.

4. By comparison with the figures dealt with here, Hooker is a faithful follower of Thomas Aquinas; one should not assume, however, that Hooker merely transmits Thomistic doctrine to Anglicanism. Some differences in moral theory are brought out in D. Westberg, "Thomistic Law and the Moral Theory of Richard Hooker," *Proceedings of the American Catholic Philosophical Association* (1995).

5. *Institutes* II.2.22, trans. Ford Lewis Battles (Philadelphia: Westminster Press, 1960).

6. Calvin says:

There is imprinted on their hearts a discrimination and judgment by which they distinguish between what is just and unjust, between what is honest and dishonest . . . not of the power to fulfill the law, but of the knowledge of it. . . . There is then a certain knowledge of the law by nature, which says, "this is good and worthy of being desired; that ought to be abhorred." [*Commentary on Romans,* 2:15]

7. *Inst.* II.8.1.

8. Ibid.

9. *Inst.* IV.20.15

10. Ibid.

11. Ibid.

12. *Inst.* IV.20.16; cf. Aquinas, *Summa Theol.* I-II. 95.2, and D. Westberg, "The Relation Between Positive and Natural Law in Aquinas," *Journal of Law and Religion* 11 (1994-95): 1-22.

13. McNeill, "Natural Law in the Teaching of the Reformers."

14. Heinrich Bullinger, *The Decades of Heinrich Bullinger,* 2d decade, ed. T. Harding (Cambridge, 1849), sermon 1, 194.

15. Ibid., 194-95.

16. Ibid., 205.

17. Ibid., 197.

18. Ibid., sermon 7, 340.

19. Ibid.

20. Ibid., 343:

Now mark that politic laws do for the most part consist in three especial and principal points—honesty, justice, and peace. Let laws therefore tend to this end, that discipline and honesty made be planted and maintained in the commonweal. . . . Let law forbid all uncleanness, wantonness, lightness, sensuality, and riotousness, in apparel, in building, in bibbing and banqueting. . . . Let adulteries, whoredom, rapes, and incests, be put to exile. . . . Briefly, whatsoever is contrary to honesty and seemliness, let it by law be driven out and rejected.

21. See Keith L. Sprunger, *The Learned Doctor William Ames: Dutch Backgrounds of English and American Puritanism* (Urbana:University of Illinois Press, 1972).

22. See Daniel Westberg, "Thomistic Law and the Moral Theory of Richard Hooker," in *American Catholic Philosophical Quarterly* 68 (1994), Supplement, 201-14.

23. William Ames, *Conscience and the Cases Thereof,* V.i.100.

24. Ibid., I.ii.5.

25. L. W. Gibbs, "The Puritan Natural Law Theory of William Ames," *Harvard Theological Review* 64 (1971): 57.

26. Ames, *Conscience and the Cases Thereof,* V.i.108

27. Ibid. 103-4.

28. Ibid., 107.

29. Hugo Grotius, *On the Law of War and Peace,* trans. Kelsey (Oxford:Oxford University Press, 1925), 38-39.

30. See Heinrich Rommen, *The Natural Law: A Study in Legal and Social History and Philosophy,* trans. T. R. Hanley (St. Louis, 1947), 71 n. 4.

31. Grotius, *On the Law of War and Peace,* Proleg., 11.

32. Ibid., 12.

33. Ibid., 12-13.

34. See John F. Kilner, "Hurdles for Natural Law Ethics: Lessons from Grotius," *American Journal of Jurisprudence* 28 (1983): 159-60. This is also the conclusion of Rommen in *The Natural Law,* 71, and of A. H. Chroust, "A Summary of the Main Achievements of the Spanish Jurist-Theologians in the History of Jurisprudence," *American Journal of Jurisprudence* 26 (1981): 112-24, who pointed out that this verdict on Grotius was promulgated by Pufendorf and is "without foundation in fact and wholly unjustified and unjustifiable" (120).

35. Grotius, *On the Law of War and Peace,* Proleg., 23.

36. Kilner, "Hurdles for Natural Law Ethics," 153-54.

37. See Rommen, *The Natural Law,* 72-73.

38. Emil Brunner, *The Divine Imperative,* trans. O. Wyon (London, 1937), 271.

39. Ibid., 272-73.

40. Ibid., 629-30, n. 8.

41. Emil Brunner, *Justice and the Social Order,* trans. M. Hottinger (New York: Scribner's, 1945), 95.

42. Ibid.

43. Ibid., 89-90.

44. Ibid., 86.

45. Ibid., 89.

46. Ibid., 92.

47. See Paul Henry, "Types of Protestant Theology and the Natural Law Tradition" (Ph.D. thesis, Duke University, 1970), 260.

WILLIAM EDGAR

1. This statement may very well be from Suárez, not Grotius.

2. See the classic study by Richard S. Westfall, *Science and Religion in Seventeenth-Century England* (New Haven: Yale University Press, 1958).

3. Francis Turretin: *Institutes of Elenctic Theology*, vol. 1, trans. George M. Giger, ed. James T. Dennison, Jr. (Phillipsburg, N.J.: Presbyterian and Reformed Publishing, 1992), 6-16.

4. Richard A. Muller, *Post-Reformation Reformed Dogmatics*, vol. 1 (Grand Rapids: Baker, 1987): 190. Nor do they view natural law as providing any kind of basis for positive morality (191-92).

5. Jacob Vernet, *Traité de la vérité de la religion chrétienne, tirée du latin de M. J.-A. Turretini* (Geneva, 1730, 1785).

6. See the study on this drift in the American context by James Turner, *Without God, Without Creed: The Origins of Unbelief in America* (Baltimore and London: Johns Hopkins University Press, 1985).

7. W. R. Everdell, *Christian Apologetics in France, 1730-1790: The Roots of Romantic Religion*, Texts and Studies on Religion, vol. 31 (Lewiston, N.Y.: Edwin Mellen Press, 1987).

8. I am going to focus on the Reformed version of biblical theology. There has been a noted Neo-orthodox version of biblical theology, but that is another subject.

9. Geerhardus Vos, *Biblical Theology* (Grand Rapids: Eerdmans, 1948), 13f.

CHAPTER 4

"The Concept of Rights in Christian Moral Discourse"

JOAN LOCKWOOD O'DONOVAN

1. Two useful bibliographical guides to this philosophical and theological literature on rights are found in John Warwick Montgomery, *Human Rights and Human Dignity* (Dallas: Word Publishing, 1986), and Charles Villa-Vicencio, *A Theology of Reconstruction: Nation-building and Human Rights* (Cambridge: Cambridge University Press, 1992).

2. In post-war Catholic social thought, Pope John XXIII's celebrated endorsement of human rights in *Pacem in Terris* (1963) was followed by the Roman Synod of Bishops' *Message Concerning Human Rights and Reconciliation* (1974) and the work of the Pontifical Commission Justitia et Pax entitled *The Church and Human Rights* (1975). Pope Paul VI's sparing use of the concept, more remarkable on the account of his humanist progressivism, has been reversed by Pope John Paul II (in, e.g., *Sollicitudo Rei Socialis* and *Centesimus Annus*), whose thought about rights has stimulated a considerable secondary literature.

Not surprisingly, the WCC has led the Protestant ecumenical world in a wholehearted advocacy of human rights since its collaboration on the Universal Declaration of Human Rights in 1948. Conferences at St. Pölten (1974) and Nairobi (1975) produced two collections of papers: *Human Rights and Christian Responsibilities*, vols. 1-3 (Geneva: World Council of Churches, 1975), and David M. Paton, ed., *Breaking Barriers: The Official Report of the Fifth Assembly of the World Council of Churches* (London, 1976), 119-41. At its centenary meeting of 1977, the World Alliance of Reformed Churches accepted a theological apology for human rights prepared by Jürgen Moltmann, including it and his earlier commissioned study, together with other Reformed essays, in A. O. Miller, ed., *A Christian Declaration on Human Rights* (Grand Rapids: Eerdmans, 1977). Within the Calvinist covenantal tradition, a more reserved and subtle theological underpinning of human rights came from Jacques Ellul, who sustained a soteriological and Christocentric focus to the concept, in *Le Fondement Théologique du Droit* (Neuchatel/Paris, 1946), 34-45, 56-65, 78-93.

The Lutheran World Federation comes closest to departing from the ecumenical approval of human rights. Under the leadership of Heinz Eduard Tödt and Wolfgang Huber, its studies collected in *Theological Perspectives on Human Rights* (Geneva: Lutheran World Federation, 1977) and in Jörgen Lissner and Arvil Sovik, eds., *A Lutheran Reader on Human Rights* (Geneva: Lutheran World Federation, 1978) exhibit a tendency to theological suspicion of subjective rights as a construction of secular political reason. However, despite their occasionally penetrating criticisms of the conceptual content of rights, these Lutheran thinkers do not appear to regard the language of human rights as more problematic than other political-ethical languages with which the gospel message finds points of contact.

3. It may be objected that neither the ruler's creation of law nor the subject's possession of rights was a novel theme, the former composing a permanent strand of Roman imperial legal theory and the latter a central feature of the feudal system. The key point, however, is that throughout the earlier medieval period these themes were theoretically contained by or subordinated to the political models and principles found in the Bible as authoritatively interpreted by the Church Fathers with the help of Platonic and Stoic philosophy. They took on controlling political significance only with the assimilation of Aristotelian thought, the consolidation of territorial kingdoms and the papal church, the proliferation of self-governing city states, and the theoretical integration into the Roman juristic framework of, on the one hand, feudal customs and ideas and, on the other, corporational principles and concepts.

4. The papal case was developed in four bulls between 1323 and 1329: *Ad conditorem canonum, Cum inter nonullos, Quia quorumdam mentes,* and *Quia vir reprobus,* collected in C. Eubel, ed., *Bullarium Franciscanum,* V (Rome, 1898). A concise presentation of the case is found in Gordon Leff, *Heresy in the Later Middle Ages,* vol. 1 (Manchester: Manchester University Press, 1967): 238-55.

5. See Leff's summary of John XXII's argument in *Quia vir reprobus,* in *Heresy,* 247. Richard Tuck rightly considers this assertion about Adam an important move in the history of natural property right theory, in *Natural Rights Theories: Their Origin and Development* (Cambridge: Cambridge University Press, 1979), 22.

6. The Franciscans perpetuated the Augustinian tradition of viewing private property and ownership as a post-lapsarian institution dependent on political authority, and common use of things without possession or proprietorship as characterizing the state of created innocence.

7. It should be emphasized that the non-proprietary "right of use" *(ius utendi)* defended by Ockham was a right under natural law that entitled the individual to use things necessary for bodily sustenance. It was, therefore, a statement of the Franciscan concept of *simplex usus facti,* of a simple use of necessities involving none of the legal relationships to them *(proprietas, possessio, usufructus, ius utendi)* and the freedoms and privileges entailed in these relationships (e.g., to alienate or donate the material thing or seek legal redress for wrongful deprivation of it). In my judgment, Tuck is not as explicit as he could be in distinguishing Ockham's natural *ius utendi* from the legal

188 NOTES TO PAGES 147-157

ius utendi rejected by the Franciscans, although he clearly intends the distinction. The key point is that Ockham formulated the Franciscans' "simple use" as a natural right or "licit power," not without theological and juristic precedents, it must be said, but with an influential (and perhaps novel) schematic emphasis.

8. Among Gerson's followers discussed by Tuck are Conrad Summenhart, John Major, and Jacques Almain, who spread Gersonian thought from the influential nominalist centers of Tübingen (Summenhart) and Paris (Major, Almain). Tuck also draws attention to the role played by Gerson's conciliarist contemporary Pierre d'Ailly. See Tuck, *Natural Rights Theories*, 24-31.

9. Ibid., 25-27.

10. Luis de Molina, *De Iustitia et Iure*, 1 (Mainz, 1614): cols. 162-63, and Francisco Suárez, *De Legibus ac Deo Legislatore* (Coimbra, 1612), vol. 1 of the Carnegie Endowment edition (Oxford: The Clarendon Press, 1944): 160; translation in vol. 2:279, cited in Tuck, *Natural Rights Theories*, 54, 56.

11. Suárez, *De Legibus*, 1:205; 2:381, cited in Tuck, *Natural Rights Theories*, 56.

12. Molina, *De Iustitia*, 3: col. 399; Suárez, *De legibus*, 1:11; 2:30-31, cited in Tuck, *Natural Rights Theories*, 53, 55.

13. Hugo Grotius, *De Iure Belli ac Pacis* (Paris, 1625), 4-5 (I.I.IV-VIII); translation in J. Barbeyrac, ed., *The Rights of War and Peace* (London, 1738), 3-6, cited in Tuck, *Natural Rights Theories*, 74-75.

14. C. B. Macpherson, *The Political Theory of Possessive Individualism: Hobbes to Locke* (Oxford: Oxford University Press, 1962), 3.

15. Thomas Hobbes, *Leviathan*, ed. M. Oakeshott (London: Macmillan, 1962), 103.

16. Ibid.

17. Ibid., 103-33.

18. Ibid., 110-11.

19. Macpherson, *Political Theory*, 140

20. Ibid., 142-43.

21. Ibid., 144-46, 150.

22. Ian Shapiro in *The Evolution of Rights in Liberal Theory* (Cambridge: Cambridge University Press, 1986) gives a lucid and convincing account of the indispensability of individual autonomy to Locke's workmanship model of property acquisition. The worker's ownership of the products of his work depends on his prior ownership of his action, and such ownership is synonymous with the subject's freedom to act apart from the obligations of the natural law (90, 96). In drawing our attention to Locke's analogy between divine and human workmanship, Shapiro illuminates the continuity between Locke and Pope John XXII's understanding of divine and human *dominium,* and, more generally, the importance of the nominalist stress on divine sovereignty for the Western development of property right.

23. Thomas Paine, *The Rights of Man* (New York: Dolphin Edition, 1961), 306.

24. Twentieth-century rights theorists such as D. D. Raphael and Wesley N. Hohfeld distinguish categorially a "right of action" or "liberty" from a "right of recipience" or "claim-right," the former expressing the subject's freedom in action from obligation to act and the latter correlating with the obligation binding the action of others vis-à-vis the subject. Both theorists would agree that the first right normally entails the second, legally but not logically. See D. D. Raphael, "Human Rights, Old

and New," in Raphael, ed., *Political Theory and the Rights of Man* (London: Macmillan, 1967), 58-61, and Wesley N. Hohfeld, *Fundamental Legal Conceptions* (New Haven: Yale University Press, 1919).

25. The logic of the conceptual transition from right as property to right as positive entitlement may be discerned in Shapiro's exposition of John Rawls's attempt to synthesize negative like certain and positive welfare principles, in Shapiro, *Evolution of Rights*, chap. 5.

26. This contract was alternatively called the "contract of submission."

27. The covenantal themes of Frankish capitularies and coronation oaths greatly influenced later imperial and royal pacts and oaths. The pervasive influence of feudal structures is also discernible in the formal expressions of bilateral obligations between monarchs and their secular and spiritual magnates. See John W. Gough, *The Social Contract: A Critical Study of its Development* (Oxford: Oxford University Press, 1957), chap. 3.

28. The most comprehensive and detailed presentation of sixteenth-century theories of political and social compact is found in J. W. Allen, *A History of Political Thought in the Sixteenth Century* (London: Methuen, 1928; new ed., 1961). Both sixteenth- and seventeenth-century theories are treated quite thoroughly in J. H. Burns, ed., *The Cambridge History of Political Thought 1450-1700* (Cambridge: Cambridge University Press, 1991), and more briefly by Gough in *The Social Contract,* chaps. 5-9.

29. Johannes Althusius's synthesis of organic Aristotelian and legal contractualist models of political society is particularly interesting, not least for its profound influence on later European Christian political thought and institutions. In his *Politics* (1603, 1614) he described the encompassing political community as a federation of private, civil, and public associations, each of which is a corporate structure of right and rule formed by a compact according to divine (revealed and natural) law. This synthetic model fostered a corporatist conception of rights as belonging to a plurality of social office-holders, offices and rights being attached to every communal institution.

30. Shapiro, *Evolution of Rights,* 197-98.

31. An impressive example of this argument is provided by John Finnis in *Natural Law and Natural Rights* (Oxford: The Clarendon Press, 1980), chap. 8.

32. Shapiro, *Evolution of Rights,* 146.

33. In a dramatic change of mind, Jacques Ellul in 1981 unequivocally repudiated subjective rights on theological grounds and proceeds to a devastating social analysis of the culture of "rights." He described the attrition of charitable and generous impulses, the breakdown of mutual trust and openness, the atomistic moralism and rigidity throughout society, and as well the stultification of governmental administration and judicial arbitrariness resulting from "la diffusion, [le] triomphe de la relation juridique dans les relations humaines" ("Recherches sur le droit et l'evangile," in L. L. Vallauri and G. Dilcher, eds., *Cristianesimo Secolarizzazione e Diritto Moderno: Per la Storia del Pensiero Giuridico Moderno,* no. 11/12 [1981], 115-39).

Index of Names

Abimelech, 70
Abraham, 3, 90
ACLU, 94
Adam, 3-4, 21, 65-66, 69, 85,
    100-102, 147
Aeterni Patris, 15
Alaric, 141
Althusius, 152
American Revolution, 144, 148,
    150, 165
Ames, William, ix, 104, 109-11,
    114, 116-17, 119
Anabaptists, 72
Anglicanism, 104
Aquinas, Thomas, vii, viii, 5-8, 16,
    18, 33, 35, 41-48, 91-92, 96,
    102, 104, 106, 109, 111, 113-14,
    133, 169
Aristotle, Aristotelian, 46, 48, 51,
    103, 131
Arkes, Hadley, 166
Arles, Second Council of, 5
Arminius, 111
Athens, 167
Augsburg, 31
Augustine, Augustinian, 18, 39, 46,
    100, 112, 129, 141, 144, 147

Bacon, Francis, 109, 120, 134

Balthasar, Hans Urs von, 3
Barmen Declaration, 36, 79
Barth, Karl, 2-3, 26, 34-36, 41, 47,
    52-55, 58, 77-80, 117-18, 124,
    128, 140, 167
Barth, Peter, 54
Beethoven, Ludwig van, 22
Benedictines, 102
Bernardin, Cardinal Joseph, 14
Bernard of Clairvaux, 21
Beyerhaus, Gisbert, 51, 73, 78
Biblical Theology Movement, 125
Biden, Joseph, 29, 137-38
Bloom, Allan, 167
Bohatec, Josef, 52, 78
Bonaventure, St., 24
Bork, Robert, 137
Bouwsma, William, 54
Boyle, Robert, 121, 131
Brunner, Emil, ix, 52-55, 73, 78-
    80, 104, 114-17
Brunner, Peter, 54
Bullinger, Heinrich, ix, 104, 107-9,
    114, 116-17, 119

Calvin: Constructive Revolutionary
    (Graham), 79
Calvinism, 97, 111, 116
Calvin, John, viii-ix, 21, 51-102,

191

104-7, 111-20, 122, 124, 129-30, 133

Calvin's Doctrine of the Knowledge of God (Parker), 54

Calvin und das Recht (Bohatec), 52, 78

Canada, 137

Charleton, Walter, 121

Chicago, University of, 1

Chrysostom, 62

Church Dogmatics (Barth), 2

Church Fathers, 3, 29, 33, 46, 47

Cicero, 51, 62, 71

Cistercians, 102

City of God, The (Augustine), 141

Civil War, 165

Closing of the American Mind, The (Bloom), 167

Cochrane, Arthur C., 51-52, 54, 79

Cold War, 79

Common Sense Realism, 123

Communism, 11

Company of Pastors (Geneva), 82

Confessing Church, 78

Confessions (Augustine), 112

Conscience and the Cases Thereof (Ames), 109

Corinthians, I and II, 126-27

Corpus Reformatorum, 77

Cottier, Georges, 22

Dabney, Robert Lewis, 92

Daneau, Lambert, 122

Darkness of Atheism (Charleton), 121

Davies, Samuel, 92

Decalogue, 3, 15, 22, 51-52, 67, 73, 75, 80, 91-92, 110-11, 119

De Cive (Hobbes), 9

Declaration of Independence, 94, 134-35

Declaration on Human Rights, U.N., 169

Decretum (Gratian), 5

De Graaf, S. G. 125

De Homine (Hobbes), 9

De iure belli ac pacis (Grotius), 111

del Val, Merry, vii

de Molina, Luis, 147

Descartes, René, and Cartesian thought, 11, 16, 121

Deuteronomy, 57

Divine Imperative, The (Brunner), 114

Doumergue, Émile, 52, 78

Dowey, Edward, 54, 79

Du Moulin, Pierre, 122

Dworkin, Ronald, 14, 165-66

England, 143

Enlightenment, 9, 28, 123, 135, 146

Enoch, 3

Ephesians, 126

Erasmus, 39

Erlangen school, 35

Ethics and Public Policy Center, vii, x, 43

European Community, 143

"Evangelicals and Catholics Together," 79

Evangelium Vitae, viii, 14-15, 30, 34, 95, 169

Eve, 3, 66, 69, 102

Everdell, W. R., 124

Fall, the, 8, 44, 58, 61, 65-67, 75, 85, 99, 110-11, 114, 125

Faventinus, Johannes, 10

Fifth Lateran Council, 82

Finnis, John, 158, 162

Franciscans, 146

Freemasonry, 11

French Revolution, 144, 165

Fuchs, Joseph, 17-18, 34

Gaffin, Richard B., 125

Gaudium et Spes, 18, 98, 170

Genesis, 10, 12, 23, 25, 30, 37, 65; chap. *1,* 61, 63-64, 125; *chap. 2,* 3, 21, 23; *chap. 3,* 24

Geneva, 77

George, Timothy, 54

Georgetown University, 42

Germany, 52

Gerson, Jean, 147
Gloede, Günter, 54, 73
Göttingen, 77
Graham, Fred, 79
Gregory of Nyssa, 3, 24
Grotius, Hugo, ix, 104, 111-17,
119, 132, 33, 140, 152

Hebrews, 129
Hobbes, Thomas, and Hobbesian
thought, 9, 98, 132, 134, 144,
148, 153, 165, 167
Hooker, Richard, 104, 109
Humanae Vitae, 12, 17
Hume, David, 98, 120, 131
Hurons, 102

Incarnation, 4
Indiana University, 42
Institutes of Justinian, 5
Institutes of the Christian Religion
(Calvin), 21, 56, 71, 79-81, 85,
99-100, 106
Institutes, The (Turretin), 122
Israel, 37-38

Japan, 43
Jefferson, Thomas, 29
Jenson, Robert, 35
Jeremiah, 63, 127
Jerusalem, 167
Jesuits, 102, 147, 152
Job, 67
John XXII, Pope, 146
John XXIII, Pope, 13
John Calvin and the Church
(George), 54
John Paul II, Pope, viii, 12, 14-15,
19-26, 30, 32, 42, 95-97,
166-67, 169
Judah, 69
Judiciary Committee, U.S. Senate,
29
Julian Act, 5
Justice and the Social Order
(Brunner), 115

Kant, Immanuel, and Kantian
thought, 9, 11, 38, 46, 144
Kilner, John, 113
King, Martin Luther, 29
Klempa, William, 54
Knitter, Paul, 39
Knowledge of God in Calvin's
Theology, The (Dowey), 54

Lang, August, 51
Leibniz, G. W., 123
Leiden, University of, 111
Leo XIII, Pope, 15
Levellers, 148-50
Libertines, 72
Lincoln, Abraham, 29
Little, David, 54, 79
Locke, John, 9, 14, 134, 144, 148,
150, 165, 168, 170
Loyola University, 41
Lutheranism, Lutherans, 31-32,
35-36, 81, 104, 107, 144
Luther, Martin, viii, 31, 38-39, 78,
87, 167

Machiavelli, 132
Macpherson, C. B., 149, 168
Man and the State (Maritain), 167
Marburg, 77
Maritain, Jacques, 14, 115, 167
Mary, 21
Matthew, 21, 23, 108
Mayflower Compact, 134
McNeill, John T., 55, 79
Melanchthon, 62
Melchizedek, 3
Metaphysics (Aristotle), 48
Middle Ages, 102, 120
Missio Redemptoris, 40
Montaigne, 88
Moore, G. E., 120, 131
Mosaic Law, 8, 10
Moses, 3-4
Mt. Sinai, 75
Muller, Richard A., 123
Murray, John Courtney, 14, 28, 89

National Council of Catholic
   Bishops, 16
National Socialism, 78
Nazis, 36
Netherlands, 109
Newsweek, 128
Niebuhr, H. Richard, 38
Niebuhr, Reinhold, 115
Niesel, Wilhelm, 54
Noah, 3
Nozick, Robert, 154

Occam (Ockham), William of,
   112, 147
Oman, 69
Original Unity of Man and Woman
   (John Paul II), 23
Overton, Richard, 148-49
Oxford, England, 143

Paine, Thomas, 150
Parker, T. H. L., 54, 79
Paul, Apostle, 7, 56, 126-27, 136,
   141
Paul VI, Pope, 12
Peck, Thomas, 92
Pelagianism, x, 7, 39, 96-97, 127
Pelagius, 39, 102
Pharisees, 21
Pilgrims, 82
Pinckaers, Servais, O.P., 15
Plantinga, Alvin, 138
Plato, Platonic, 71, 110
Plymouth, 82
Presbyterians, 9, 92
Princeton Theological Seminary,
   49, 125
Princeton University, 93
Proverbs, 63
Psalms, 24, 61, 63
Pufendorf, Samuel, 116-17, 120,
   133
Puritans, 109, 152

Rahner, Karl, 39
Rawls, John, 154

Ray, John, 121, 131
Reformation, 55, 77, 87, 115, 117,
   119, 122
Reformers, vii, 53, 55, 75, 84, 92,
   103, 107, 112
Reid, Thomas, 123
Renaissance, 76
Ridderbos, Herman, 125
Roman Empire, 140
Romans, *chap. 1,* 36, 53, 97, 108;
   chap. 2, 6, 24, 55-56, 58, 105;
   chap. 8, 126; *chap. 12-15,*
   126-27, 141
Rome, 141
Rousseau, Jean-Jacques, 9, 14, 144
Roy, Cardinal Maurice, 12-13, 16,
   41

Satan, 21, 38, 67
Schaeffer, Francis, 136
Schilder, Klaas, 125
Schoenberg, Arnold, 22
Scholastics, 82, 104, 112, 117, 148
Scotus, 41
Second Vatican Council, 15-16,
   18, 34, 39, 98, 104
Selden, John, 153
Seneca, 62, 71
Sentences of Peter Lombard
   (Aquinas), 8
Shapiro, Ian, 153-54
Simon, Yves R., 1
*Social Teachings of the Christian
   Churches, The* (Troeltsch), 78
Sources of Christian Ethics, The
   (Pinckaers), 15
Stoics, 46, 112, 114
Suárez, Francisco, 147, 152, 167
Summa Contra Gentiles (Aquinas),
   43
Summa Theologiae (Aquinas), 5, 8,
   16, 43
Supreme Court, 29

Ten Commandments, *see*
   Decalogue

Tertullian, 3-4, 6, 42
Theater of His Glory, The: John Calvin and the Natural Order (Schreiner), 81
Thessalonians, I, 126
Thielicke, Helmut, 103
Thomas, Clarence, 29, 137-38
Thomism, 11, 35, 45, 103, 133
Thurneysen, Eduard, 77
Torrance, T. F., 54, 79
Tradition of Natural Law, The: A Philosopher's Reflections (Simon), 1
Troeltsch, Ernst, 40, 51, 78
Turretin, François, 122-23
Turretin, Jean-Alphonse, 123

Usefulness of Experimental Philosophy (Boyle), 121

Vatican II, *see* Second Vatican Council

Veatch, Henry, 42
Veritatis Splendor, viii, 2, 16, 19-22, 26, 30, 34, 37, 92, 95
Vos, Geerhardus, 125-26

Weber, Max, 167
Westminster Confession, 91, 96
Westphalia, Peace of, 120, 134
Whigs, 152
Wisdom (book of), 42
Wisdom of God Manifested in the Works of Creation, The (Ray), 121
Witsius, Herman, 122
Wolff, Christian, 123
Wolterstorff, Nicholas, 138
World War II, 14, 36, 41, 79, 93, 115
Wycliffe, John, 162

Zurich, 107
Zwingli, 87, 107